# A Small Steps Guide to Goal Setting and Time Management

by
Louise Tondeur

Emerald Guides
www.straightforwardbooks.co.uk

Emerald Guides

© Copyright Second Edition Dr Louise Tondeur 2023

ISBN: 978-1-80236-213-8

Author Photograph by Sarah Barnsley

Cover Design by BW Studio Derby
Text layout by Frabjous Books

The right of Louise Tondeur to be identified as author of this work has been asserted by her in accordance with Copyright, Designs and Patents Act 1988

All rights reserved. No reproduction, copy or transmission of this publication may be made without written permission. No paragraph of this publication may be reproduced, copied or transmitted save with the written permission or in accordance with the provisions of the Copyright Act 1956 (as amended). Any person who does any unauthorised act in relation to this publication may be liable to criminal prosecution and civil claims for damage.

Whilst every care has been taken to ensure the accuracy of this work, the author or publisher cannot accept responsibility for loss occasioned by any person acting or refraining to act as a result of any statement contained within this book.

# Contents

## PART 1: GOAL SETTING

**Chapter 1: Small Steps to Goal Setting** .................... 2
- Small steps in a nutshell .................... 2
- About this chapter .................... 2
- Small steps to goal setting: an introduction .................... 2
- Keeping a journal .................... 6
- What is a goal? .................... 6
- Initial exercises .................... 11

**Chapter 2: The Small Steps Method in Action** .................... 13
- About this chapter .................... 13
- Case study .................... 13
- Mindset exercises .................... 15

**Chapter 3: Goal Setting** .................... 18
- About this chapter .................... 18
- Goal setting exercises .................... 18
- Action lists .................... 26

**Chapter 4: What it Takes to Get Where You Want to Go** .................... 27
- About this chapter .................... 27
- How to work out which small steps you need to take .................... 27
- Prepare to succeed .................... 29
- What's getting in your way? .................... 32
- More on confirmation bias .................... 34
- Doing your research .................... 35
- What do you need to achieve *first* or *instead*? .................... 37

**Chapter 5: Reality Check** .......................................................... **41**
About this chapter ..................................................................... 41
The Alcoholic's Prayer ................................................................ 41
Risk assessment ......................................................................... 43
The impossible dream paradox .................................................. 44
Dream big ................................................................................. 46
Testing your goals ..................................................................... 48

**Chapter 6: The Science of Happiness** ...................................... **50**
About this chapter ..................................................................... 50
Happiness Pioneers ................................................................... 51
Different happiness measures .................................................... 53
Different kinds of happiness ..................................................... 54
Making other people happy ...................................................... 56
Support from others, supporting others .................................... 58

**Chapter 7: A Review of Goal Setting Methods,
Including the Goal-Free Method** ............................................. **63**
About this chapter ..................................................................... 63
Productivity, work or sales goals ................................................ 64
The habits of success ................................................................. 65
Focus / avoiding distraction ...................................................... 67
Using life roles or the whole self ................................................ 68
Channelling mistakes and perseverance ..................................... 70
Being journey-focused ............................................................... 72
Commonalities and concluding thoughts ................................. 74

**Chapter 8: Motivation. What Is It? Do You Need It?** ............ **76**
About this chapter ..................................................................... 76
What is motivation? .................................................................. 76
How to develop more motivation .............................................. 79
You don't need motivation ........................................................ 83
Motivation doesn't exist! ........................................................... 84
Key motivation blind-spots ....................................................... 87
No need to get motivated .......................................................... 88

# CONTENTS

## PART 2: TIME MANAGEMENT

### Chapter 9: Small Steps to Time Management ........ 92
About this chapter ............92
Small steps time management: an introduction ............92

### Chapter 10: Productivity and Time Management ............... 98
About this chapter ............98
What does productivity mean anyway? ............98
How to prioritise ............102
Productivity advice............103

### Chapter 11: Small Steps Time Management In Action ........ 109
About this chapter ............109
Time management examples............109
Time management basics............110
Time management specifics ............113
Practice exercises ............116

### Chapter 12: I Wanted to Change the World But I Could Never Find the Time: Time Management and The Overworked ............ 118
About this chapter ............118
Rhythms and hotspots............118
1440 minutes............120
10080: the number of minutes in a week ............122
525,600 minutes and beyond ............124

### Chapter 13: Circadian Rhythms ............ 127
About this chapter ............127
What are circadian rhythms? ............127
Larks and owls............128
My 5am writing habit............128
Working with your circadian rhythms ............130
Cultural expectations for days of the week............131

## GOAL SETTING AND TIME MANAGEMENT

Months of the year .................................................................. 133
Circadian Rhythms Activities ................................................. 134

### Chapter 14: Set It Up, Break It Down, Make It Easy ........... 137
About this chapter ................................................................... 137
Set it up .................................................................................. 137
Break it down ......................................................................... 142
Break it down example: raising money ................................... 143
Break it down example: writing a novel .................................. 146
Using subheadings to break down tasks .................................. 147
Make it easy ............................................................................ 151
Case study: Set it up, break it down, make it easy ................... 153

### Chapter 15: Make It Count, Keep It Balanced, Think Whole Picture ............................................................ 155
About this chapter ................................................................... 155
Make it count ......................................................................... 155
Keep it balanced ..................................................................... 160
Think big picture .................................................................... 164

### Chapter 16: Balanced Planning ........................................... 167
About this chapter ................................................................... 167
The hour-by-hour approach .................................................... 167
Timetabling ............................................................................ 170
Small steps to balanced time management .............................. 172
Balanced planning on trial ...................................................... 173

### Chapter 17: Small Adjustments ........................................... 174
About this chapter ................................................................... 174
Project management ............................................................... 174
Systems and routines .............................................................. 175
Filing ...................................................................................... 177
Money .................................................................................... 178
Decluttering your stuff ........................................................... 179

CONTENTS

**Chapter 18: Small Tools** ............................................. **181**
    About this chapter ..................................................... 181
    Focus on the small stuff .............................................. 181
    Looking back on your niggles and bugs ..................... 183

**Chapter 19: Small Ways to Keep Check** ................... **185**
    About this chapter ..................................................... 185
    Check in ..................................................................... 185
    Communicate ............................................................. 186
    Collaborate ................................................................. 187
    Collect ........................................................................ 187
    Compost ..................................................................... 187

**Chapter 20: Bibliography and Resources** ................ **189**

# PART 1
# GOAL SETTING

# Chapter 1: Small Steps to Goal Setting

### Small steps in a nutshell
You can take a task, however daunting, and break it down into smaller and smaller steps until it becomes manageable. You can do small things in your everyday life to allow you to achieve what you want to.

### About this chapter
This chapter introduces the Small Steps Method. I start by telling you more about me and about how this book works. Then I'll ask you to begin to think about yourself and your values and aspirations and show you the ten small steps principles. The rest of the chapter includes the basics of keeping a journal, and a definition of what a goal *is* and what a goal *isn't*. It finishes with a brief introduction to Abraham Maslow's *hierarchy of needs,* and then you'll get some practical exercises for you to try straightaway.

### Small steps to goal setting: an introduction
*Who am I?*
I'm a writer – of stories mainly – and I lecture in Creative Writing for the University of Brighton and the Open University.

Rewind back to 2011, we had a small baby at home, we were living in rented accommodation in London, and wondering if we would ever be able to afford to buy a house. It seemed impossible, out of reach, and out of our league. We watched other people – who had, by design or accident, bought before prices in London went crazy – buying gorgeous apartments at high prices and it was easy to feel gloomy, especially as we didn't know what the future would hold.

We were talking about this in our lounge one day – our landlords had a thing for zany wallpaper, so imagine bright blue walls and one

## 1: SMALL STEPS TO GOAL SETTING

flowery brown one – and it suddenly occurred to me that *if we could let go of the outcome* but at the same time take tiny steps towards our goal, we might one day get what we wanted. The opposite – doing nothing because it was too overwhelming and it seemed impossible – definitely wouldn't get us our dream, whereas taking small steps might. I don't simply mean the linear steps towards buying a house that you can read all over the internet, and in guidebooks and brochures produced by the banks. These steps also had to tackle our attitude towards the whole thing, what Carol Dweck calls 'mindset'.

I had already been researching goal setting and time management for a first-year undergraduate course I taught and had collected lots of materials together for them. What I read fascinated me. I've always struggled with executive functioning skills – although I didn't yet have my dyslexia diagnosis and didn't know I was neurodivergent at the time – and reading up on how to get organised was a personal journey of discovery too. I gradually realised that I loved reading about this stuff and that I needed to learn more about it.

So, I did what I always do when presented with something I need to learn: I wrote about it. Every Friday afternoon when my wife took our son swimming, I gathered together everything I had on time management, did lots more reading and research, and wrote about what I called the Small Steps Method. This became the book you are holding in your hand – the first Small Steps Guide.

Fast forward to 2023, and I'm sitting in my writing shed at the bottom of the garden. We've been living in our own house near Brighton for ten years. Taking small steps worked for us. It wasn't a magic wand and letting go of the outcome was key – but we took the small steps anyway. Buying a house was the first time I'd articulated the small steps to myself, but we had already been using the Small Steps Methods for other big things in our life, as you'll discover. What you're reading is the revised edition of the book, with two brand-new chapters and an updated list of books and resources on goal setting, time management and finding lasting happiness.

*About this book*
This book is designed to do four things:

- You'll be introduced to the Small Steps Method.
- You'll learn how to set personal, value-led goals.
- You'll learn the principles of time management.
- You'll get a list of resources to help you take things further.

The book is divided into two halves: goal setting and time management. This introduction gives you a basic overview of the Small Steps Method. Both sections of the book elaborate on it. The advice in the first section is designed to fit any kind of goal setting, whether it relates to a habit, personal ambition, your career, your finances, a charity or business, or a group of people with a shared dream.

*Discovering your goals: An overview of you*
First I'd like to invite you to do an overview of you. Stop and do this now. What's good about being you? Take a moment to appreciate yourself. What are your dreams and ambitions and your hopes for the future? Is there anything you'd like to change? Are there any skills you'd like to develop?

- In your journal, come up with a list of your personal values.
- Pick three core values to work with for now. We'll come back to personal values later.

*The Small Steps Method*
The Small Steps Method is about taking a task – any task – and breaking it down into small steps. It doesn't matter what that task is, the same principles apply. Here are the small steps principles. The rest of the book is dedicated to showing you how to apply them to goal setting and time management.

1. Small steps are small. Break down a task until you get to something you could easily achieve today.
2. Small steps are specific and concrete. Make the small steps as

## 1: SMALL STEPS TO GOAL SETTING

down-to-earth and measurable as possible if it suits your goal.
3. Small steps don't cost a fortune. Do as many free steps as possible first. Financing a project can also be broken down into small steps.
4. Small steps are just like footsteps: Take one small step and take another small step after it. Keep taking small steps.
5. Small steps are just small steps. They don't rely on luck, on other people, or on results.
6. Small steps don't necessarily go in a straight line. Actions don't have to lead directly to the next action, as long as they all relate back to a value or a goal.
7. Take lots of small steps, especially at the beginning.
8. Turn up. Small steps require you to get off the sofa, unless lying on the sofa is important to your goal.
9. Once you've prepared, you can do small steps without even thinking about the bigger picture.
10. Small steps deserve to be appreciated. Pause at regular intervals to acknowledge your progress and to keep in check. Keep a record.

*What you need to do to understand and follow the Small Steps Method*
Throughout this book, I suggest that you do some exercises. This is a common theme of the Small Steps Method – small practical exercises that:

- help you to be more aware of your life, your values and your goals.
- help you to access a technique or idea.

As you go along, do the exercises in a journal; I recommend using a paper-based journal, but the digital equivalent is also fine. I suggest that you do these exercises in a journal *so that you can collect them in one place and look back over them*. A small notebook will be useful for some of the other suggestions, so you can carry it around.

By the way, some of the exercises are repeated, getting more advanced or more detailed each time. This is deliberate: so that you're introduced to a concept first and then given time to work on it. The exercises won't all be relevant to you. Pick those you're interested in and leave the others.

## Keeping a journal
*What is a journal?*
Outside of the exercises, you may find it helpful to jot down your thoughts in your journal while you are working towards your goals. This particularly relates to small steps principle number 10: *small steps deserve to be appreciated.* Your journal is a good place to record a commentary on the process. It's also a place to record your feelings, dreams and ideas. You can use it like a scrapbook too. There are various other reasons to keep a journal:

- It's a record of your progress in a particular goal or project, focusing on challenges and setbacks, successes and unexpected pleasures resulting from the journey you've decided to undertake.
- It's a place to keep practical ideas and suggestions.
- Use it for inspiration. Save inspirational images, words and snippets of text to help you to visualise where you want to go.
- Get it out of your head and onto the page. You can use a journal for self-expression – to vent in whatever way you want to.
- It's good for gratitude. Research has shown that those people with a gratitude practice are happier and mentally healthier. A quick way to start is to jot down one thing you are grateful for each time you journal.
- Chapter three includes a number of goal setting activities. Once you've worked through them you'll have a complete list of the goals you want to achieve. Include this list in your journal in a prominent place so you can refer back to it.

*Who writes about journaling?*
Journals have become increasingly popular in recent years. If you're interested in taking journaling further, have a look at the resources section for more.

## What is a goal?
*Defining 'a goal'*
Before you start setting goals, it's useful to figure out exactly what a goal

## 1: SMALL STEPS TO GOAL SETTING

means. For the purposes of this book, a goal is:

- concrete and specific (or at least can be phrased this way). You will never know if a goal is achievable – or *even something you actually want to do* – unless you make it concrete and specific. Concrete means you'll know if you've achieved it. It's something you could actually do in real terms. Specific means getting down to the details of what you would have to do to achieve the goal. It's not general or vague.
- something you want to achieve. It's odd when you think about it but a lot of us go round with (usually rather vague and non-specific) goals that come from what other people expect of us, or that we have heard somewhere are good ideas. Let go of it if you don't really want to do it.
- attached to a reason (even if it's 'because I fancy it'). One danger with goal setting is that we make up goals to do with something we're not really interested in, just because it's become a habit. A goal has a reason attached to it – you know why you want to do it.
- often time-limited (or at least can be turned this way). Many writers on goal setting agree that we can tell whether we've achieved a goal or not by using a timeframe. This is scary because it means committing to do something by a particular date, which is why many of our goals remain unformed in our heads and we never let go of those we don't really want to do. However, not all goals need to be time-bound – we'll come back to this later.
- achievable (but it can be a challenge). This seems obvious at first sight but it's the chief paradox of goal setting advice. We're told to dream big or even to dream the impossible. Some even seem to imply that we don't need to take any action – just thinking about it enough will make it happen. A goal needs to be challenging *and* achievable.

And now, just to make sure, let's look at what a goal *isn't*:

- What you think you *should* do. A goal isn't guilt-laden; a goal is about what you *want* to achieve: sometimes a subtle difference, sometimes a huge one.

- What other people think you *should* do: it's impossible to dispel other people's expectations entirely – especially when they are close friends or relatives – but your heart will never be in it if you follow society's agenda or a parent's or your boss's or next-door neighbour's. Make sure they are *your* goals.
- What you *could* do: perhaps you *could* train to cross the Sahara Desert, win a pie eating contest, or hike in the Andes – but do you want to? Idiomatic goals (used in the media as short-hand for high achievement) like writing a novel, running a marathon, swimming the Amazon and climbing Kilimanjaro can catch us out – it's ok if you don't.
- Inflexible or set in stone: a myth put about in some goal setting self-help books is that we must do anything and everything to strive towards our goals. Not true! They might change. You might change.
- A promise or a guilt trip. You can change your mind; if you don't achieve your goal you've learnt something along the way.

*Do you need a goal?*
Stop and do this now, using your journal:

1. Spend some time making a list of the skills you have – not only those you are paid for. Now make a list of skills you would like to improve. Refer back to this list as you work through the rest of this chapter. We'll return to this list again later.
2. Write these headings in your journal: career, community, health, hobbies, family, finances, friends, learning, love, spirituality, travel, leisure, social life. Do any of these parts of your life stand out as particularly significant?

*Aspirations and dreams v. what I need right now*
There are two kinds of goals. Seemingly impossible dreams on the one hand and the perhaps more mundane or everyday things I need to change right now. Aspirations and dreams are expressed as if they are way off

# 1: SMALL STEPS TO GOAL SETTING

in the future whereas 'things I need now' goals are immediate. You'll probably have *both* kinds of goals.

*Shared goals*
Many goals are not individual ones. You may have the same goals as work colleagues or your life partner. Equally your goals might conflict. Even when a goal is an individual one it will still have an impact on others. Make an effort to understand any shared or conflicting goals.

*Overlapping goals*
Goals generate other goals. Some goals automatically generate *overlapping* goals: goals I need to achieve at the same time. For example: 'I want to start a family' not only has an impact on others, but it also brings financial goals with it, which might generate career goals: perhaps 'I want a steady job' or 'I want to work freelance.' It might also generate overlapping health goals. For example: 'I'm going to give up alcohol.'

*Overlapping and overwhelming?*
Overlapping goals can feel overwhelming. Deal with them by breaking each one down into small steps. Then take small steps towards each goal every week. I recently found the notebook where we planned small steps towards achieving our goal of having a family. Seeing it brought back all those overwhelming feelings about the prospect of going through IVF, the cost, emotional and financial, the thought of having to lose weight and get fit, the idea of having to inject myself! The *only way* I could do it was by breaking it down into manageable steps. Then I looked at my son and realised we'd done it! It didn't matter about those difficult feelings – we did it anyway. You know what? Even if it hadn't worked I would still be glad that I had tried.

*Separate goals*
Once you break down a goal into steps, it might generate completely separate goals: goals I need to achieve first. For example, if you needed to do another qualification before enrolling on a college course or if

you needed to boost your confidence before applying for a volunteer position. Separate goals are easier than overlapping goals because you can manage them one at a time.

When you realise you have a set of separate goals, it helps to work out a medium-term timeframe for yourself: *I will have achieved my goal in X amount of time.* Doing so on paper also allows you to note any time constraints. Time constraints can turn separate goals into overlapping goals.

Stop and answer this question now, in your journal: do you have shared, overlapping, conflicting or separate goals?

*Your hierarchy of needs*
In the 1940s, psychologist Abraham Maslow – the first to coin the term 'Positive Psychology' – expressed all the things human beings need as a hierarchy, called the *hierarchy of needs*. It's usually drawn as a pyramid and has five levels. At the bottom are physiological or biological needs, followed by safety, love / belonging and esteem, with self-actualisation at the top. Maslow argued that each level of need must be satisfied before those above it, and so on, up the hierarchy. He argues that without fulfilling our basic needs – having enough food to eat or a safe place to live – we can't look after our 'higher' needs that might include achieving our goals. Another way of putting this is that we all have physical, psychological / emotional, social, cultural and spiritual needs. Neglecting one kind of need will impact on the other.

*Food chain*
For example, food is a physiological need – on the bottom rung of Maslow's hierarchy. Do you eat breakfast? Do you keep your blood sugar level balanced? Do you eat enough fruit and veg? You don't need me to tell you that all of these things affect our mental health and our physical health, and therefore have an impact on how we manage our daily routine. Long term they create a chain reaction and have an impact on whether we achieve our goals or whether achieving our goals makes us happy. Following Maslow's idea of a hierarchy, we wouldn't neglect

## 1: SMALL STEPS TO GOAL SETTING

healthy eating or a good night's sleep because we're chasing a deadline or under pressure in another area of our lives. If you think about it, it also doesn't make sense to argue that we *don't have enough time* to eat healthily, for instance.

### Initial exercises
*The many parts of your life*
Take a moment now to stop and think about the many parts of your life – all the things you do with your time. It helps to begin thinking this way because it's a theme that we'll return to later. Make a quick list. Then leave it for a while. Have a cup of tea or drink of your choice before returning to your list. Is there anything you'd like to add? Any life part that's missing? We'll come back to this at the beginning of chapter three.

*Things I'll do before or after I'm / Things I've always wanted to do but…*
At the back of your mind, you could be harbouring the idea that you'll do X before you reach a certain age, or after you lose a stone, or before you get married, or before you have children, or after the kids leave home, or after you retire – some version of 'I'll do that thing when'. Most of us also have a vague idea of things we've always wanted to do and a 'but' stopping us from doing them. Taking time to write them down begins to make them less vague so we can either let them go or take action.

Make a list of yours in your journal now by filling in the blanks in the following:

I must do_____before I'm_____.

Once I_____, I'll do_____.

When I_____, I can_____.

*Small steps practice*
Try the following three-part exercise in your journal in order to practise breaking a task down into small steps:

1. Flowchart. In your journal, create a series of boxes in the shape of a flowchart. Now *chart the steps* you need to drink a glass of water. Be as specific as possible.
2. Picture. This time *draw* the steps you need to take to drink a glass of water.
3. Write it. Now *write down* the small steps.

*Small ways to keep check*
If you do the practical exercises step-by-step as you work through this book you'll automatically be keeping a check on your progress. Here are some other ways to keep on top:

- A Grateful List. Stop for a moment and make a list of things you are grateful for right now. This is a real mood lifter and helps to put your goals in perspective. Repeat this regularly.
- Review your small steps regularly – on the train to work, for instance.
- For a more structured approach, do this once a day if you can and incorporate them into your daily routine. Or review your small steps once a week and add them to a schedule for the rest of the week – on Sunday evening or Monday morning, for instance.
- The most important thing is that you choose an approach that works for you.

*What's next?*
Now you're familiar with the basics of the Small Steps Method, let's look at a case study so you can see how it works in practice.

# Chapter 2: The Small Steps Method in Action

### About this chapter
This chapter gives you an example of the Small Steps Method in action, using a case study, followed by some mindset exercises designed to get you to use both *divergent* and *convergent* thinking.

### Case study
*Rhonda, the trainee radio journalist*
Here's the goal setting example that uses the Small Steps Method. It's about a small steps novice. Let's call her Rhonda. Rhonda's goal is to become a radio journalist. You may have no interest in radio journalism. Bear with me. This is simply a way to practise thinking in small steps.

If you were Rhonda, which small steps might you take? Here are some possible answers:

- Write down your goal and make it specific: *By the time I am X, I have a regular slot as a sports reporter on a major radio station.*
- Use the internet to research routes into your chosen career and volunteer opportunities.
- Go to the local library to browse their careers resources.
- Find out about local colleges in your area.
- Download more information about journalism courses.
- Attend an open evening.
- Fill in an application form.
- Look up local hospitals online to see if they have a radio station.
- Email three hospital radio stations.
- Post a request for contacts on a social media network.

## GOAL SETTING AND TIME MANAGEMENT

*What happens next?*
While studying journalism at college, Rhonda volunteers at a hospital radio once a fortnight. She meets someone there who invites her to do work experience at a local radio station. While doing work experience, she meets someone who works as a sports reporter. He gives Rhonda advice about how to approach potential employers. She sends a sample of her slot on the hospital radio show to an acquaintance. One of the people she's contacted so far emails to tell her about a job as a stand-in traffic reporter. She gets the job as the stand-in traffic reporter and….

*The Small Steps Method in action:*
Here's how the actions Rhonda takes fit with all ten of the small steps principles.

1. All of Rhonda's small steps can be set in motion in a few minutes or a few hours.
2. All of the steps are specific, measurable, down-to-earth and concrete.
3. All of the initial steps can be done for free (or nearly free).
4. All of these steps simply require you to identify and complete the next small step *even if it seems as though nothing much is happening.*
5. None of these steps happen through luck. While 'meeting someone who works as a sports reporter' might seem like luck, just as you're more likely to get on a bus if you stand at a bus stop, you're more likely to meet a sports broadcaster if you're at a radio station! Although Rhonda is supported and advised by other people, each step requires her to be proactive herself.
6. She doesn't wait for one of the steps to yield results before trying another small step. This is a common stumbling block and important for goal setting, especially in the initial stages. You'll notice that one step doesn't necessarily lead to the next, but it always relates back to the original goal.

## 2. THE SMALL STEPS METHOD IN ACTION

7. Although each step is small, our prospective radio journalist goes for multiple approaches to her goal at first: research, a college course, volunteering, work experience, asking for contacts.
8. All of the steps require some action: they require her to turn up.
9. She's clearly thought carefully about how to achieve her goal and broken it down into small steps. After that, some steps she can just do without thinking about the big picture too much – like turning up at the library or the open evening or emailing the radio stations.
10. We don't know if she pauses at regular intervals to appreciate her progress or whether she keeps a record. We *can* tell, however, that the whole process will work much better if she does do these things. This level of awareness will have a real impact on whether she achieves her goal.

While 'become a radio journalist' might have seemed impossible to Rhonda before she started, now it's broken down into very specific steps it feels achievable.

### Mindset exercises

Carol S. Dweck is a Professor of Psychology at Stanford University. Her bestselling book, *Mindset: How You Can Fulfil Your Potential*, discusses the difference between a "fixed mindset" and a "growth mindset". People with a "growth mindset" use challenges and setbacks as a chance to learn, and Dweck demonstrates how we can develop such a mindset ourselves. The mindset exercises that follow challenge you to adopt a "growth mindset" when working on your goals.

*Why do these exercises?*
These exercises involve both *divergent* and *convergent* thinking. Do them even if they feel silly, strange or impossible: that's a sign that you're thinking differently.

GOAL SETTING AND TIME MANAGEMENT

*Life categories*
Stop and do this now in your journal. Think of this exercise as a practice. We'll build on it in the next chapter.

1. Choose ONE part of your life to focus on from: career, community, health, hobbies, family, finances, friends, learning, love, spirituality, travel, leisure, social life. Write it as a heading in your journal.
2. Write down one thing you want to achieve in that part of your life. Do a quick check: if you had done this thing, how would you feel? Can you visualise yourself completing it? Is this something you want to achieve in 1 year, 5 years, 10 years or 20 years? Rewrite the goal to make it as concrete and specific as possible.
3. Make a list of any actions related to the goal that:
   a. can be done in 5 mins.
   b. can be done in half an hour.
   c. can be done in a day.
4. Honesty time. Look back over your notes. Why haven't you done the things on your list already? Be honest. It will help you to discover blocks and also whether you genuinely want to achieve the goal.

*Draw pictures*
1. Pick another area of your life from the list above. Draw an image representing what it looks like now and what it will look like in the future. Take your time, but you don't need to be a great artist for this to work.
2. Use colour. Make the images as big and bold as possible.
3. Give each picture a caption.
4. Review what you've done by writing some notes in your journal.

*Trip to Europa*
1. Scientists think there could be life on one of Jupiter's moons: under the frozen sea that covers Europa. You're going to plan a trip there!

## 2. THE SMALL STEPS METHOD IN ACTION

2. Draw a flowchart. On one side of the paper draw a box and inside the box write your goal *as if you have already achieved it*, in the present tense. For example: 'I am swimming in the oceans of Europa.'
3. Work back across the paper, drawing boxes to represent each step you would need to take to achieve this goal. Use blank boxes to represent gaps in your knowledge.
4. Create a list of gaps in your knowledge and turn this into a research plan.
5. Review what you've done in your journal. You're probably not going to achieve this goal or carry out the research unless you work for Nasa! The aim of this activity is to practise working out the small steps you need to achieve *any* seemingly impossible goal.

*What's next?*
We've seen how the Small Steps Method works, and you've tried some exercises to get you thinking creatively – and to put you in the mood for thinking about your goals. In the next chapter, you're going to create a list of goals to use during the rest of your work on this book.

# Chapter 3: Goal Setting

### About this chapter
This chapter takes you through several goal setting activities. Work through them in your journal and you'll end up with a complete list of goals you want to achieve. Once you've completed the exercises in this chapter you'll have generated lists of actions related to your goals – it's these actions that you'll be breaking down using the Small Steps Method.

### Goal setting exercises
We'll go through several goal setting exercises now, designed to help you to think about your goals from different angles.

*Taking inspiration from the Wheel of Life*
Drawn as a circle with segments for each part of your life, the Wheel of Life is a commonly used tool in coaching, and there are various iterations of it. A wheel will typically have categories such as health, work, money, relationships etc. included. The original 'Wheel of Life' is attributed to Paul J. Meyer who set up a training company to encourage people to achieve their goals in the 1960s – today we would call him a life coach.

In the first mindset exercise from the previous chapter, I suggested career, community, health, hobbies, family, finances, friends, learning, love, spirituality, travel, leisure, social life as life categories, inspired by this common coaching tool. We're going to develop that first mindset exercise from chapter two now, taking longer over it this time.

1. Use those same subheadings, leaving out any that aren't applicable. Feel free to tweak them or invent your own. If you need inspiration, search for versions of the Wheel of Life online.
2. Write down at least one thing you want to achieve in each area.

## 3: GOAL SETTING

3. Now answer the following in your journal: if you had done these things, how would you feel? Can you visualise yourself completing these goals? Are these goals you want to achieve in 1 year, 5 years, 10 years or 20 years? Rewrite the goals to make them as concrete and specific as possible.
4. Make a list of any actions related to these goals that:
   a. can be done in 5 mins.
   b. can be done in half an hour.
   c. can be done in a day.
5. Honesty time. Look back over your notes. Why haven't you done the things on your list already? Be honest. It will help you to discover blocks and also whether you genuinely want to achieve these goals.

*Your life, your goals, your roles*
You're going to create your own bespoke list of *life roles* in your journal. This time be specific about your own life, rather than using the generic categories of a typical life wheel.

1. Come up with as many life roles as possible by answering these questions.
   a) What do you do with your time? Don't evaluate. Just make a list. For example, I like baking, I sing in a choir, I teach Creative Writing.
   b) What roles or parts do you play in a typical day? For example, I'm a mother, a partner, a daughter, a teacher and a writer.
   c) Check that these life roles are all relevant to you right now.
2. Strike out any area where you know you don't want to set goals. For example, baking is important to me as a hobby, but I don't have any baking goals.
3. Decide on *the most important role for goal setting* right now. Focus on one role at a time.
4. Make a list of what you would like to achieve in this area of your life. Note any shared goals. Decide which are aspirations

## GOAL SETTING AND TIME MANAGEMENT

or big dreams and which are more everyday goals. Now take a break.

5. Visualise yourself achieving each goal. Take time out to do the following. Picture yourself achieving this goal in detail and experience how you would feel. If this visualisation makes you feel excited or apprehensive or enthusiastic, this is a goal you're interested in. If it makes you feel uninspired or you can't be bothered to do this part of the exercise, strike this goal off your list – it's a 'should' or a 'could' and not a genuine goal. If visualisation doesn't chime with you, make notes instead.
6. *Even if it feels impossible*, set a time frame. When will you achieve each goal? Is this something you want to achieve in 6 months, 1 year, 5 years, 10 years or 20 years?
7. What would half-way look like? For example, if your goal is to be debt-free in five years' time, what will you have achieved in 2 and a half years?
8. Rewrite each goal to make it as concrete and specific as possible.
9. Take one goal at a time. Make a list of any actions related to the goal that:
    a) can be done in 5 mins.
    b) can be done in half an hour.
    c) can be done in a day.
10. Honesty time again. Look back over your notes. Why haven't you done the things on your list already?
11. Repeat this process until you've recorded your goals for all the life roles you want to include.
12. Do a final check to make sure you are not setting goals for anything you're not interested in.
13. Select the goals you want to work on. If you've come up with a large number of goals, pick the ones you are *most* excited by and make sure you have a balance by including different parts of your life.
14. Repeat steps 12 and 13 in a week's time. This is an important part of the process.
15. Make yourself a list of goals.

## 3: GOAL SETTING

*Charting your goals*
1. Review your notes so far.
2. Create a table on a computer or draw yourself a chart in your journal. A computerised version makes it easier to adjust. Give it six columns.
3. Now add column headings for the goal, the life part related to the goal, the reason for your goal, the time limit, and how you will reward yourself. Also include a column for what the half-way point will look like.
4. Add all of the goals you've selected to your chart.
5. In your journal, record any emotions attached: excited, daunted, bored, reluctance, eager.
6. Write down any overlapping, shared, conflicting or separate goals.
7. For each goal, ask: *What's the very first action?*

*Think big*
This exercise is designed to expand your thinking. You don't need to know how you would achieve these big goals – just have fun with it.

1. Look over the chart you just created.
2. Look at one goal. Use your imagination to make the goal bigger.
3. In your journal, write down a bigger goal. Now get even bigger.
4. Keep going. Get as big as possible. Write down a bigger goal each time.
5. Note any emotions attached as before.
6. Repeat this exercise for all of the goals on your list.
7. This exercise is designed to trick your mind into daring to dream big, by revealing what you'd do if money, time and responsibilities were no object.
8. Come back down to earth and adjust your chart. Do you need to make any of your goals bigger?

Now we'll repeat and elaborate on the other mindset exercises from before, again spending longer over them.

GOAL SETTING AND TIME MANAGEMENT

*Get ready to play*
This is a playful way to think about your goals. If you thought colouring in was for pre-schoolers think again! Give yourself enough time to fill the paper you chose. Working on this activity with other people is enlightening, too.

Use the largest piece of paper you can. A roll of paper you can cover the floor or table with would be ideal or you could buy A2 sheets or even stick together plain A4 sheets of paper. Get some big coloured pens to use. (Hint: NOT the kind that smell bad. Our olfactory system has a real impact on our emotional memory.)

1. Draw pictures. Think about each part of your life. Draw two images for each one: how it looks now and how it will look in the future. Take time over it but it doesn't matter if it doesn't look 'right' because you also get to label each picture with a caption. Be as messy as you like. Doodling is encouraged.
2. Play music. While you write and draw, play something uplifting.
3. Use colour. Try to get through all the colours you have. Don't stick with one. Keep going until you have filled the paper with colourful images and words.
4. Review what you've done. Get your journal and write some notes. If you love what you've produced, keep it. Stick it on the wall or keep it safe somewhere. If it's all too silly, put it in the recycling. This might seem like an obvious or petty suggestion but it's important advice: too often we feel as if a task isn't finished simply because we're holding onto some physical aspect of it.

*Creating flowcharts*
Most people who do this activity in one of my workshops come away realising that what had been a vague half-formed idea is actually achievable. They also soon discover whether they want to put in the effort necessary to achieve their goal – and whether it's really a goal at all. There are two possible approaches here. Have a go at both.

Have a time limit. Work in twenty-five-minute bursts, with a five-

## 3: GOAL SETTING

minute rest after each. (This is an example of Francesco Cirillo's Pomodoro Technique in action. Have a look in the resources section for more.)

Equipment: as before, find the largest piece of paper you can. Get some big black or blue marker pens to use.

1. Draw a flowchart as neatly and methodically as you can. No doodling. Draw a box for one of the things you're involved in right now on the left-hand side of the paper.
2. Draw subsequent boxes across the paper with a next step in each one – depending on your goal in that area. (You can repeat this for other things you're involved in – that's why you're working on a large sheet of paper!)
3. Write a possible next step in each new box. Don't evaluate at this stage, just write the steps down. Make each step start with a verb. If it's still an unformed or vague idea, write it down anyway, but use 'research' as your verb. You're not committing yourself yet. You're still playing with possibilities.
4. Each box may have a number of possible next steps, but draw one line of steps at a time, then go back and create another line of steps if you like. It might feel like a hard task to keep coming up with more steps: that's the point. Be as specific as possible each time.
5. Someone wise once told me that if you continue on the path you're on, you'll get to where you're going. Include that possibility in your diagram. Draw a line showing the path of least resistance or what you'll end up doing if you don't go in a new direction. *Very often this isn't a bad thing,* but it helps us to make conscious decisions.
6. Above and below each step, create implication boxes. *Evaluating* implications can put us off before we've even considered how a goal might work. Don't evaluate yet. Simply list the implications in boxes or bubbles above and below each step.

Let's imagine someone who is working as a teacher. That's one of the things she's involved in right now, so she would write that in a box on the left hand-side. The first possible next step could be 'research teaching abroad'. The step after 'research teaching abroad' might be 'go to careers show'. 'Research options to work abroad' might have an implication box that reads 'leaving family behind for a year or take them with me.'

Need inspiration? Look back at the case study in chapter two involving the prospective radio journalist. What implications would she have to consider? Financial ones, if she has to pay for the course, and practical ones if she needs to find childcare, for instance.

*Flow in the other direction*
I promised you two versions of this technique, so now you're going to repeat the flowchart exercise. This time, start from where you want to be and do the following:

1. Draw a box for each one of the things you know you want to achieve within a certain time limit on the right-hand side of the page.
2. Write these as if they are true, in the present tense. For example, *I own and run my own vineyard in the South of England.*
3. In this approach, you're going to take steps backwards from your achieved goal to where you are now. Make a list of backwards steps in your journal first to get them in the right order. For example, 'buy a vineyard' might seem like the next backwards step from 'own and run my own vineyard' but remember you said run as well. You'll need some specific set up steps for your vineyard too.
4. Take a step back and draw a box for it. Then repeat. Keep going until you get back to where you are now.
5. You can draw 'implications boxes' around the steps as appropriate. An obvious one in this example is financial. Doing your flowchart this way is harder and forces you to confront gaps in your knowledge, giving you very specific areas to research. Don't be afraid to leave empty boxes for this purpose.
6. Give yourself multiple options. This is why you need a big

## 3: GOAL SETTING

piece of paper because now you are allowed to become more divergent! Use your imagination. Go in and add more options to the flowchart. Make them a different colour.

Next, review what you've done. Get your journal and write some notes on your flowcharts. As with the earlier goal drawing exercise, if you love the results of the flowchart exercise, keep them. Stick them on the wall or keep them safe somewhere. If not, record what you need, then put them in the recycling. Let them go.

Next we're going to have a go at narrowing down your goals. This is a crucial part of the process.

*Warren Buffett's 5/25 rule*
Warren Buffett's goal setting advice is fairly well-known, so there are lots of articles about it online, especially on websites giving productivity tips. I like James Clear's blog post on the idea, as it suggests that you play along as he tells the story – so he turns the anecdote into a practical exercise.

Buffett told his personal pilot, so the story goes, who was called Mike Flint, to write down 25 bucket-list goals and to circle those that spoke to him the most. Then he had Mike cross off all the other 20 and avoid them. Try it yourself! According to Buffett, these 20 now comprise your 'Avoid-At-All-Costs list'. You don't give them any attention until you've done your top 5.

*Have a go at Warren Buffett's 5/25 exercise now:*
- Reflect on the goals you've recorded in your journal so far.
- Take time to write out 25 goals on a new page – perhaps some you've been working with already and some new ones. Make these bucket-list level goals – ones that really count.
- Circle or underline 5 of them.
- Cross out, delete or discard 20 of them.
- Decide on the first few small steps for the 5 that remain.

**Action lists**

Now you're looked at your goals, here's how to get your to-do list – or Small Steps Action List – up and running.

*Creating and using action lists*

By the end of this section of the book, you'll have created a list of small steps relating to your goals. These will be specific actions that you'll then be encouraged to schedule in a morning, afternoon or evening slot, or to incorporate into your daily, weekly or monthly routine.

You can handle these actions by keeping a to-do list, or Small Steps Action List. This can be as rough or as systematised as you like. A Small Steps Action List is a working document. Edit your list or lists as you complete some steps and add more. Either:

- Keep one main Small Steps Action List containing all of your small steps. You can keep everyday tasks on this list too. Keeping one Small Steps Action List and combining it with your regular to-do list works well if you want to thoroughly integrate your goals into your daily life. Keep a copy of your list somewhere very obvious: stuck on the fridge or on a noticeboard where you work.

OR:

- Keep a separate Small Steps Action List for each goal, perhaps in colour-coded box files, which you refer to when you've put aside time to work on a particular project. This works well if you want to keep your projects compartmentalised. Add steps to an everyday to-do list when you need to. This is the one you stick on the fridge or noticeboard.

*What's next?*

You've been through various goal setting exercises to help you to look at your goals from different angles. You should now have a list of goals to work with. In the next chapter, you'll come up with the small steps you need to make them happen. We'll also look at some of the things that might get in the way, and how to handle them.

# Chapter 4: What it Takes to Get Where You Want to Go

**About this chapter**
This chapter is all about what you need to do to make your goals a reality. We start by looking in more detail at how to work out your small steps. Then we look at preparing to succeed: what you can do to lay the foundations mentally and practically. Next you'll find out how you can identify the blocks that are stopping you from achieving your goals, and how to do your research. Finally, we do a goal check: do you need to achieve something else first or even something else *instead*?

**How to work out which small steps you need to take**
*Small steps to drinking a glass of water revisited*
Look back at the exercise called 'small steps practice' in chapter one. At the time, you wrote down the steps needed to drink a glass of water. Use them to practise the three Rs of the Small Steps Method: record, reason, revise.

1. *Record* the small steps you think you'll need. In the 'drinking a glass of water' example, you already did this in a flowchart, a picture sequence and written steps. You could also 'relate' the steps to a friend over a cuppa.
2. *Reason* with yourself: do I need to go any further back or get more simple, more basic or more specific?
3. *Revise* your small steps: rewrite them, adding any extra detail you need. Imagine you were explaining the action to someone else. Do the steps need revising?

*You need to go further back than you think you do*
Look back at what you wrote in your journal in response to this exercise

in chapter one. Did you turn on the tap or open a bottle? Did you open the cupboard and get out a glass? Where did you imagine drinking it? Did you drink sparkling or still? Did you add lemon? Did you find some sand to make the material for your glass? Did you find someone who knows about glassmaking to help you? Did you employ a water-diviner? Or did you gather your neighbours together to dig a well? How did you purify the water? Just as you could keep taking a step back when it comes to drinking a glass of water, you can keep taking steps back with *any task you need to perform.*

*You need to get smaller than you think you do*
How specific did you go with the glass of water task? How long did you turn the tap on for? How clean was the glass? Just as you could keep getting more specific when it comes to drinking a glass of water, you can keep getting more specific with any task you need to perform, until you've literally written (or drawn!) yourself instructions. The harder – or more unfamiliar – the task, the closer you need to get to a list of simple written instructions. If you don't know how yet, add a research step, and make it small.

*Points to remember:*
- If you think you're stuck you might need to take a few more steps back. Write down the task, take a step back, and another, and another until you get to the *simplest appropriate step*. Make it something you could do today.
- Or you might need to get even more specific. This is true with complicated or unfamiliar tasks, including tasks that are *emotionally* complicated or unfamiliar.
- Anything vague or unformed, anything you don't know how to do – add the word 'research' and leave a gap to fill in later.

*Context is everything!*
The people at the charity Water Aid describe themselves as follows: "Our mission is to transform lives by improving access to safe water, hygiene

## 4: WHAT IT TAKES TO GET WHERE YOU WANT TO GO

and sanitation in the world's poorest communities." Drinking a glass of water is simple – no need to break it down into steps. But for the people Water Aid helps every day, drinking water is far from straightforward. Your context will:

- inform how far back you need to go to get to your first small step
- allow you to understand the specifics of your project.

For example, it would have been physically impossible for me to run a marathon just before having our baby! When I first wrote this book, a young woman called Amber Miller had recently featured in the news because she had run the Chicago Marathon and had her baby – a healthy little girl called June – shortly afterwards. We were both new mums, but our contexts, and our levels of fitness, were different.

*Consider your environment*
Stop and do this now. Take some time to think about the environment, people, spaces, resources and things that surround you. Do they help or hinder you in achieving your goals and in your day-to-day life?

## Prepare to succeed

Let's continue to look at the Small Steps Method in more detail. There are some practical things you can do to increase your chances of success.

*Set yourself up for success*
I give you the seven 'C's of setting up:

- Carry a small notebook and pen: It could be digital or physical. Make it your companion. Carry it with you so that you can jot down ideas as they occur to you.
- Cabinet or crate? Sort out your filing. Living with your papers in a mess is a big roadblock. Take a weekend to put everything you need in order, to store it somewhere easy to access and to recycle (securely) what you don't need.
- Create (or identify) a space where you can work. Ideally this will

be somewhere permanent that's just for you but even a tray next to your bed with a pen and notebook on it is a start. Ask people to treat it with respect.
- Clear the clutter. Another big roadblock is clutter. Take another weekend to identify what you really need. Is there anything you can sell online? Or anything you can list on recycling or swapping websites like freecycle? Or anything you can donate to charity? Have a look at the resources section for more on decluttering.

*The story of your success*

In this exercise, you look at how you have succeeded before and turn it into a story that you can use as a model for future achievements.

1. Think about a project or an area of your life where you succeeded, where you saw it through from beginning to end, where you were proud of yourself.
2. Can't think of anything? Ask someone close to you for an example. Or ask yourself: what one thing could you do right now to make things better? Drink a glass of water, for instance. Go and do it! Use that glass of water to create your success story for now.
3. Create an achievement story for yourself. Take a goal from one area of your life and over the next few days do something – just *one thing* - towards achieving it. Use whatever you achieve to create your story of success, then come back to this exercise.
4. Let the story you create be right for you. If you want to be a writer, signing up for an evening class is reason to congratulate yourself. We don't celebrate our achievements enough – especially not our small steps – and we should. A similar principle applies to people who are very driven. If you *have* run a marathon, written a novel, or climbed Kilimanjaro, celebrate it! Very driven people tend not to give themselves time to take stock after each achievement. You can do that now by writing the story of your success.

## 4: WHAT IT TAKES TO GET WHERE YOU WANT TO GO

5. Describe the story verbally to someone close to you or write it in your journal: Where did you do it? How long did it take? What research did you have to do? What state of mind were you in during the project or once you had finished? What support did you receive?

*We learn by making mistakes*
Human beings have evolved to learn by making mistakes. The process of learning requires us to try something out, if it doesn't work, we try again, perfecting our skills along the way. If you know any babies or young children you can watch them learning like this. My son tried over and over again to crawl before he learned how to do it. The same thing happened when he learnt to walk. The idea of someone criticising him each time he 'failed' to crawl or walk doesn't make any sense! But as adults this learning process gets scuppered when – because of criticism from ourselves or people around us – we give up at the first hurdle. It's been said many times that successful people aren't lucky. They just have a different attitude to failure.

*Hurdles exercise*
Stop and do this now. Identify any hurdles you overcame in the success story you wrote in your journal earlier. How did you overcome them and why? What did you do next? What did you learn from the experience?

*Just keep taking small steps*
Your attitude to failure is important, but the Small Steps Method stops it becoming a stumbling block. Let's go back to the prospective radio journalist at the beginning of the book. Rhonda emails three hospital radio stations and eventually volunteers at one. She 'fails' to get two of the volunteer positions she tries for, but it doesn't matter. One opportunity is all she needs. Instead of giving up after the first rejection, set back, or negative response, just keep taking small steps. For now, let go of the outcome.

For any task that seems too big or too complex or confusing to begin even, work out the first small step, then – without thinking about the prospect of success or failure for a moment – just work out another small step and another. You're not committing yourself to achieving them by writing them down or by taking that first small step.

*Putting your success story to work*
This is where you put past successes to work for you, so that you can use them to help you achieve your goals. In addition to the following, make time to read about other people's journeys to success. Pick people you admire and seek out any books they've written. You'll almost certainly find that the person you find inspiring didn't have a smooth ride to success; in fact, the bumps along the road were probably an important part of the journey.

1. Look back at the story of your success. What were the key things that made you keep going until you succeeded?
2. Now think about a goal you want to achieve and consider your success story. What would you need to do to apply this story to your new goal? Is there anything missing this time that you had last time?
3. When you need a boost, focus on success stories like the one you just created These stories are so powerful because they are concrete examples from your own life.
4. Have a look at the books on success and perseverance, such as *Grit* by Angela Duckworth, Carol S. Dweck's *Mindset*, *Peak* by Anders Ericsson and Robert Pool, Tim Harford's *Adapt,* or Matthew Syed's *Bounce.*

## What's getting in your way?
*Self-criticism*
It's all too easy to allow our internal critic to stop us from making progress. It trips us up because when we listen to it we don't want to learn from our mistakes. But the more you hear your internal critic, the more likely it is you're trying something new.

## 4: WHAT IT TAKES TO GET WHERE YOU WANT TO GO

*Confirmation bias*
Look down at the floor and close your eyes. Now think: "blue." Open your eyes and look around. What do you notice? Repeat the exercise with different colours. Try this before reading on.

Most people will notice the colour they thought about prior to opening their eyes. This also works with our attitudes about the world. If I metaphorically "look around" with the idea that the world is full of selfish people that's what I'll see. If I "look around" with the idea that nothing I do will succeed, my brain will obligingly look for evidence for me. This is an application of what psychologists call *confirmation bias*. To read more about confirmation bias and the other cognitive biases, including the negativity bias, check out the Very Well Mind website. The link is in the resources section.

*Identifying blocks*
Here are some exercises that should enable you to identify the blocks that stop you from taking small steps towards achieving your goals. If you lack self-confidence or you are having trouble believing in the important projects you identified in chapter three, these are particularly pertinent:

1. Spend just one journey (not if you're driving!) thinking "leaves are fascinating" or "everyone has a secret" or "people in this town are always smiling" – did you notice confirmation bias in action? See if you can pick up on any kind of *negativity bias* in your day-to-day life. We're wired to scan the world for problems so we pick up on difficulties much more easily than the good stuff – one reason why a gratitude practice is so useful.
2. You've probably heard of the saying "smile and the world smiles with you" but did you know that it is literally true? Try smiling at everyone you meet. Yes, some people won't react, but most of them will. A demonstration of the idea that it only takes a small change in attitude to start seeing the world differently!
3. Spend a week noticing your internal critic. Just observe – don't respond one way or the other. Make notes in your journal. Be

ready to laugh at it, rather than arguing with it. Remember that even the most successful people have an internal critic – it's nothing to do with how much you've achieved.

4. In your journal make a list of the things that are stopping you from making progress. This could be physical, financial, practical or emotional blocks, or knowledge gaps. Be as specific as you can.

5. Is your problem *really* your problem? Think particularly of your environment and those around you. For example, one student I taught was convinced she had writer's block. After questioning her, I discovered that her neighbours were renovating their house and she was trying to write to the sound of them knocking down walls. She had another problem too: she didn't have any confidence in her abilities. As soon as she created a quiet space to work somewhere else, her writer's block disappeared, and her confidence grew – but she had to do it that way round. This is small steps principle number 8 in action. She gained confidence from turning up in a space that worked for her and from writing one page at a time. We'll come back to this idea in the second part of the book.

It's easy to think lack of money is holding you back – but most initial small steps are free. Do them anyway.

**More on confirmation bias**
*Wishing for buses at the North Pole*
You have probably heard of the 'law of attraction'. Simply state what you want, so some proponents of this law tell us, and the universe will provide. Perhaps the law of attraction is simply confirmation bias in action. We need to *focus on* what we want and we'll find it. Stating what we want is one way of focusing on it.

Take Rhonda, the prospective radio journalist. I pointed out in chapter two that just as you're more likely to get on a bus if you stand at a bus stop, you're more likely to meet a sports broadcaster if you're at a radio station. If you stand at a bus stop and wish like mad for a bus to come,

## 4: WHAT IT TAKES TO GET WHERE YOU WANT TO GO

eventually your wish will come true. You're also *more likely* to wish for a bus at a bus stop. In fact, if you think about it, bus stops are the concrete result of a large group of people (a community) 'wishing' really hard for (wanting to use) buses. You could call that 'magic' or you could call it civilisation organising itself.

We can make confirmation bias work in our favour. It's also, logically, got to help if you think about *where* you are looking. If you wish for a bus at the North Pole, you might meet a TV crew making a documentary about polar bears or a scientist researching global warming, but it would be a very unlikely that you'd see a red double-decker London bus, no matter how hard you wished for it. So put yourself at a bus stop if you want a bus or near the North Pole if you want to research polar bears, but make sure you've got bus fair or a very warm coat first. Just like Rhonda put herself at a hospital radio station because she wanted a career in broadcast journalism, decide where you need to put yourself to make your goals a reality and find the most simple, cheapest and easiest way to get there.

*Be proactive!*
A big part of the Small Steps Method involves using confirmation bias to your advantage and that means being proactive. Focus on what you want, and as long as your basic needs are met and you'll start to notice it, just like you see pink cars everywhere if you walk near a road thinking 'pink cars'. Spend time thinking about work experience, getting published or for example eating healthily and you'll start to notice opportunities to do just that.

### Doing your research
*Identifying your research tasks*
When you created your flowcharts in chapter three, you added the word 'research' to any vague or unformed ideas. In the example, a vague idea about teaching abroad became 'research teaching abroad.' You didn't commit yourself, you simply made the first step concrete. Your reaction to that first small step gave you a clue about whether you really did want to take it further.

## GOAL SETTING AND TIME MANAGEMENT

Research can take many different forms. Spending time in libraries, bookshops and museums, going to events or training, turning up at employment fairs and networking events, chatting with colleagues or associates and using social media are all examples of research. What we don't want is for 'research' to become procrastination (or procrasti-research).

Look back through your journal. Anytime you've added 'research' to an idea, decide whether it's still important, and, if it is, highlight it and add it to a list of research tasks.

*Research exercises to get you started*
This is the point where you start working on those research tasks.

1. Take one unformed idea. Something that seems attractive but out of reach. Something you know little about. Where can you get information and advice on this particular thing? What other sources of information and advice exist? If you don't know, try some blanket networking. Ask everyone you think might be able to help – people who can be trusted with the idea of course – where you can get more information. This will generate some leads. Schedule some time to follow them up.

2. Extend your available sources of advice and information. Do you *always* use libraries first, or a search engine, or do you chat to people first? Try the alternatives. At first, take every opportunity to extend your available sources. You can do this using bibliographies in books on the topic, well-run websites and free courses, and experts in a field. Go outside your comfort zone. By 'experts' I mean people with years of experience – anyone can set themselves up as an 'expert' on the internet so check the credentials. Publication or acknowledgement from a professional body are good signs that they know their stuff.

3. Use your 'weak contacts'. The theory goes that you probably use the same resources as the people you know well. You go to similar places, like similar things and know about the same events. People you don't know very well – friends of friends of

friends (or acquaintances) – will tap into a different network involving the people *they* know well. The best way to find out about the resources available to these so-called 'weak contacts' is to ask directly. You can read more about this idea in *Connected: The Power of Social Networks* by James Fowler and Nicholas Christakis and in *Tipping Point* by Malcolm Gladwell.

4. Use social media to find 'weak contacts' and ask if anyone has any relevant expertise. If you have a lot of friends or followers on a social media network, many will be 'weak contacts' anyway.
5. Deeper research. Go back to that unformed, vague idea. You still don't have to commit long term. This time you're going to dip your toe in the water to see how you like it. Go on an introductory course, spend a day in the library reading about it, try some aspect of it that you haven't tried before, visit someone who knows a lot about it. If we *only* do internet research, we often get stuck and don't take any action. This kind of toe-dipping forces you to *do something* related to your goal.
6. Be objective. At this point, try to put aside your emotional response to this goal. Review your research so far. What are the main steps to achieving this goal? Remove emotional content or context. No implications this time. Just write down the steps. If it helps, imagine someone else is going to do it, and you're telling them how.
7. Do you need to make your goal bigger? Perhaps your research has shown up that you're limiting yourself too much. Is lack of confidence holding you back? Do you need to expand your ideas?
8. Did your research put you off? Change your mind! It's ok to go back to the drawing board. That's what research is for: to enable you to find out what you're in for if you follow this path.

## What do you need to achieve *first* or *instead*?

*What do you need to achieve first?*
Take some time to consider these questions:

- What other goals lead to your goal?
- How much money will you need?
- What qualifications do you need?
- Is 'achieve this first' standing in your way? Is it really a problem?
- Could you volunteer to gain experience or meet people?

*What other goals lead to your goal?*
This is often about getting more specific. If you want to start your own small business, 'complete a course in freelance business skills' is a goal that might lead to your goal. Take an honest look at your goals and at where you are now. If you want to publish articles and you're a complete beginner, it's not a good idea to go to the huge national and international magazines first. You could, for example, start local with your student magazine or a special interest publication.

*How much money will you need?*
Look at all related costs and how you will pay for them. Include them in a formal document, not on the back of an envelope. Look at upfront financial outlay, ongoing costs, and costs in terms of the time you'll need to invest. Next, plan to do anything that is free first before you fully commit yourself. This, of course, still has a time cost, but probably a limited one. This goes for taster courses, time spent in the library, and market research carried out amongst friends, colleagues and 'weak contacts'.

*What qualifications do you need?*
Think broadly. If you want to start a cake making business, you might already be proficient at baking cupcakes, but you'll need a certificate in food hygiene. And do you know enough about marketing to take your idea forward?

*Is 'achieve this first' standing in your way?*
Sometimes – as a form of procrastination – we tell ourselves we need to achieve something first before we can complete our goal and it's actually an excuse. You might need to jump in and have a go instead.

## 4: WHAT IT TAKES TO GET WHERE YOU WANT TO GO

*Could you volunteer?*
Nothing beats interaction with people doing what you want to do, even if it's only tangentially related. It gets you out of your usual routine and helps you to think differently, but I mention it here primarily because it's an excellent networking opportunity. In the case study in chapter two, networking opportunities came up as a result of an initially small investment of time. The illustration in chapter two is not the only way into this particular career, of course. Neither is it a straight uncomplicated path into broadcast journalism but remember small steps principle number 6: one small step does not necessarily have to lead to the next as long as they link back to the original goal. Our fictional trainee journalist seeks out a new source of information or advice everywhere she goes, and you can too.

*What do you need to achieve instead?*
This is the flipside of the previous advice on what you need to achieve first. It's a chance to review your goals once more to make sure they are exactly as you want them. Take some time to consider these questions:

- Are there any goals left on the list that you think you 'should' do?
- Do any of your goals seem tedious? Where's the fun gone?
- Could you spend more time with the people you love? Could you spend more time interacting with people?
- What would you rather do?

*Take out the 'should'*
Here's another chance to make sure that these are *your* goals and not someone else's! Where I used to work as a Creative Writing lecturer, at the start of term, we used to tell our writing students to make a list of their passions and beliefs and to write about them. Six weeks later we checked drafts of their stories. Many of them used to abandon their passions for what they thought we wanted them to write, even though they spent an entire class at the start of term learning about why writers need to write what they love. The best stories were the ones where the writer had dared to ignore the *should*. The same goes for goal setting.

*Make your goal more fun*
Does the goal seem tedious? It might be a sign that you don't really want to do it. Alternatively, you might have sucked the fun out of it as you turned it into a goal! Get back to what you really love about this area of your life. What's fun about this activity? Make a point of doing something fun – something that's related to this goal – before the end of the week. Think creatively. You might think there's nothing fun about the goal to 'become better at maths' until you play numbers games with your kids. Perhaps you don't want to turn your hobby into a business after all because you want to keep it strictly for pleasure.

*Build relationships with other people*
One of the best ways to get a sense of ourselves and what we want in life is to interact with others. Make a point of spending time doing something simple with people you love and – if you don't already – consider signing up for a leisure activity or sport that involves regular contact with other people. Once you've done that, check in with your goals and one more time (we're gearing up for the next chapter) ask yourself: what would you rather do?

*What's next?*
Now you know what your small steps are and you've identified what might get in the way, I'm going to play devil's advocate to get you to do a quick reality check – that's coming up in the next chapter. I'll also invite you to dream bigger and to test your goals using the SMART goals acronym.

# Chapter 5: Reality Check

### About this chapter
This chapter is dedicated to giving your goals a reality check. Yes, we've been trying to do that as we go along – and we had a goal check at the end of the last chapter – but here we look at reality checking in more detail. It's something that many goal setting books don't include, and it's not intended to put a dampener on your dreams. Rather, we can loosely sum up the advice in this chapter with what's become known as the alcoholic's prayer:

> "God grant us the serenity to accept the things we cannot change, courage to change the things we can, and wisdom to know the difference." – Reinhold Niebuhr

### The Alcoholic's Prayer
*Two caveats to the usual goal setting advice*
A goal assumes you want to change something in your life. The *Alcoholic's Prayer* suggests that there are some things we can change and some things we can't – some things we can set goals for and some we're better off forgetting. We need wisdom to tell the difference, or a blunt and honest look at ourselves. As I said, many books on goal setting leave out this step, urging readers to do anything in their power to achieve their goals. But there are two important caveats which they seem to forget, and they're important if you're going to give your goals a reality check:

1. Would you really do *anything* to achieve this goal? Some things may be more important than this goal. It depends what it is. You can be pretty certain that a goal like 'stop smoking by the end of the year' has almost no downsides. But would you really risk losing your friends and family or your health in pursuit of a goal?

2. In an age that celebrates so-called eternal youth and the power of the individual whilst telling us we can achieve anything we want to, there are actually some things you can't do.

*Not qualifying for the Olympics: different goals for different people*
This is the secret behind the Alcoholic's Prayer: pinpoint what you *genuinely* need or want to change. I'm never going to qualify for the Olympics. I'm not doing myself a disservice by admitting it and it doesn't matter how hard I apply myself or how many times I say positive affirmations. It's not all or nothing: almost *everyone* will improve their lives by exercising a bit more, in moderation.

During lockdown I decided to start doing yoga regularly. Looking at my son, I knew I wanted to be fit and healthy enough both to look after him and to watching him grow up. This is a big deal for me because it requires a change of attitude. For me, 'do yoga regularly' is a better goal than 'win a medal at the Olympics' or 'run the Chicago marathon.' Remember Amber Miller who gave birth after a marathon? In a BBC interview she described herself as "crazy about running". Her goals are going to be very different from mine. By the way, if you *are* a prospective Olympian: good luck!

*The wisdom to tell the difference?*
So, you're giving your goals a reality check: but how do you tell the difference between what you can change and what you can't or what you need to change and what you don't? First, get up off the sofa and *do something*. For example, I started with ten-minute beginner yoga videos on YouTube. Amber Miller spoke to a doctor before entering the Chicago Marathon. Make it something small, but something concrete. Have you:

- spoken to an expert, or if it's relevant, seen a doctor?
- been on a short course?
- spoken to someone who's already achieved it?
- done your research? Do you know enough about it to know whether this goal is for you?

- accepted your limitations?
- re-read the story of your success?

## Risk assessment
*Low risk? Jump in!*
The next stage in giving your goals a reality check is a risk assessment. Firstly, if the risks and the costs are limited, seek out the opportunity to jump in and try something for a short amount of time with low-risk involvement. For example, if you want to write comedy or screenplays, try one of the Arvon Foundation's at home masterclasses. Your risk is limited to the cost of the course, and a couple of hours of own time. Conversely, *don't* commit a large amount of time and money to a project without considering the implications. By the way, the web address for the Arvon Foundation is in the resources section.

*Reality check exercise*
Stop and do this now. At this stage of the reality check, ask yourself the following questions and write down the answers in your journal. This is your risk assessment:

- What are the financial implications? What initial steps can I take for free?
- How much will it cost if I continue? Be careful here: buying equipment or paying course fees isn't the same as achieving your goal.
- What are the risks to the other areas of my life?
- What else is important? What is *more* important?
- Are there any health implications?
- Have I discussed it with family or friends?
- Can I make the time and space?
- Is this the right thing for me now?
- Can I make the commitment?
- Why do I want to achieve it?
- Does it fit with my values?

*You might not need to commit (yet)*
My favourite quotation about commitment comes from a book about exploring:

> Until one is committed, there is hesitancy, the chance to draw back, always ineffectiveness. Concerning all acts of initiative (and creation), there is one elementary truth the ignorance of which kills countless ideas and splendid plans: that the moment one definitely commits oneself, the providence moves too. A whole stream of events issues from the decision, raising in one's favour all manner of unforeseen incidents, meetings and material assistance, which no man could have dreamt would have come his way. – W. H. Murray.

Once you commit, the magic starts to happen: the kind of magic that's a result of your determination to succeed. In the section on confirmation bias in the previous chapter, I suggested that if you close your eyes and think of a colour, when you open your eyes, you'll see that colour. Your brain looks for what you tell it to look for, so if you commit yourself, your brain will look for opportunities to fulfil that commitment. It feels like magic, and in a way it is: everyday magic. *But* you don't have to commit until you're ready. It's possible to plan first, to do your research and look at your options before committing, because that kind of preparation frees you up to think about possibilities without the frightening prospect of them becoming reality (yet). Make sure you watch out for the moment when it is time to commit. Preparation can become procrastination.

## The impossible dream paradox
*Dream the impossible or get more specific?*
This is a conundrum. We're told we need to let ourselves dream, to imagine the impossible, but honestly speaking is that really an option? Doesn't that kind of advice lead to disillusionment and cynicism? Conversely, we're told to 'be realistic' and we might have convinced ourselves not to expect too much.

Does it matter when a goal seems impossible, improbable or deluded? Here's the problem – and paradoxically those who recommend 'blue sky thinking' suffer from it too – impossible dreams are often too broad, too wishy-washy. Telling someone to 'dream the impossible' is too general: how on earth do you implement that kind of advice?

What we need, as a solution to the impossible dream paradox, is a big dose of honesty and a big dose of specificity. Often when stated specifically, a goal is no longer impossible, improbable or deluded – but it would still cost us something to achieve it. Once it's made specific we can work out that cost.

*Who says?*
Who told you the dream was impossible? If it was someone very significant – a parent, a teacher, a partner – then it is hard to be objective. How much did they know about it? How has their own life experience limited their outlook? Again, getting as specific as possible about the steps you would need to take and the time and money you would need to invest will help remove the mysticism around this apparently impossible dream. They might be right. They might not be. If you're really not sure, test it out by breaking this goal down into its component parts until you get to something you could achieve today – and taking that small step.

*What are the consequences?*
Stop and do this now. Ask yourself what the consequences of this goal are. If you had achieved this goal what would the rest of your life look like? Previously we've used Wheel of Life inspired categories and you've created your own bespoke list of life roles. Use either as a checklist to work out the consequences. Make sure that you have included the emotional consequences too.

In planning to achieve a goal you do take a risk: you risk failure. You risk having to face up to the idea that you tried but it didn't work. Usually – it depends on the goal – the journey makes that risk worthwhile. I suggest looking this one square in the face before you start but limit the time you spend doing so.

## Dream big
*Specific doubts and specific goals*

The latest life improvement guru tells us that we're 'thinking too small' or that we should 'think big' but isn't that also too general to be useful? Well, yes, but sometimes lack of confidence *does* make us put psychological barriers up. What's the solution? *Get specific* again and turn a specific doubt into an achievable goal. It's possible to learn to do all of the following things and / or to get expert help. What each one needs is an investment of *time*:

> "I could never start a cake-making business, I don't know anything about marketing".
>
> "I could never teach in Germany, I'm terrible with languages".
>
> "I'll never have a baby because the doctor says I have to lose weight first".

*The biggest outcome*

This is a practical exercise designed to help you talk yourself out of barriers such as these.

1. As a way of making 'thinking big' an achievable task, try inventing the BIGGEST outcome you can, using and reversing the doubts you have about it. Write it down. Have fun with it. We've dealt with the serious side, now you can play:

   > "My cake-making business dominates the UK market in cup cakes."
   >
   > "I learn five languages and travel around the world giving master classes in my subject."
   >
   > "I joined a weight-loss programme and have started a family. Now I give advice on weight-loss, fertility and family planning."

2. Can you get even bigger? (Notice that these get more specific as they get bigger, and not less specific.)

## 5: REALITY CHECK

"I write a series of books on cake making and become a celebrity baker, making regular appearances on television. I become known internationally as an expert in both home start-up businesses and cake decoration. I take on trainees each year who are specially chosen from the long-term unemployed."

"I am a multilingual expert in my subject, training thousands of other people to teach it. I set up academies the world over using my specially developed learning and teaching style. Many of my teachers go into schools up and down the country to start language clubs for young people."

"I have adopted four children and had two myself. I run a business helping women to get fit for pregnancy. I have marketed the franchise internationally and so far I have helped thousands of women to have a baby or to live a fulfilling life without children. I donate a portion of my profits to women running start-up ventures in the developing world."

What you'll notice when you make your dreams bigger like this is that when you get specific they no longer feel vague and unformed. You might not want to achieve the biggest version of your dream but if you've worked through the material in this book so far you should now know how to work out the small steps you'd need to follow in order to get there. You might realise that this goal isn't what you want after all, or something you're able to achieve right now. That's ok too.

3. What's the *first* small step required to realise your so-called impossible dream? Keep getting smaller until you find something you could do today.

    "My first small step was enrolling on a free course for new businesswomen run by the local council. Actually, it all started when I picked up a leaflet in the library."

    "My first small step? I have a good friend who speaks German, who went back to college. We worked out a skills exchange.

He needed help with his essays and in return he helped me to learn his mother-tongue. It all started when I invited myself to dinner and his very large family were chatting away in German."

"I'd say my first small step was making that first phone call to a weight loss counsellor. It all started when I got brave enough to pick up the phone."

## Testing your goals
*Your reality check*
Go through your list of goals. Now you've thought about reality checking, do you need to make changes? Are any irrelevant? Unachievable? Some (seemingly) impossible goals are ok – but make them as specific as you can. Have some concrete smaller goals too. If you have few big dreams, introduce some, or make one or two of your goals bigger. If you have few concrete smaller goals, set some now or make some smaller. Come back to this reality check as regularly as you need to, or whenever your goals get too general and vague.

*SMART goals*
You may have heard of SMART goals before as the acronym is used a lot in training and in the workplace. SMART goals originated in the 80s, in an article written by an American consultant called George T. Doran. The meaning of the acronym has developed over time and various coaches have altered the terminology. Doran used:

**S**pecific
**M**easurable
**A**ssignable
**R**ealistic
**T**ime-related

But many coaches now use:
**S**pecific
**M**easurable

## 5: REALITY CHECK

**A**chievable / **A**ctionable
**R**elevant
**T**ime-bound

Often adding an 'e 'and 'r' to spell 'SMARTER' as follows:

**E**valuated
**R**eviewed

Others have changed the terms to make their advice about goal setting more dynamic. **S**pecific and **M**easurable don't usually change – suggesting most coaches think the first two steps are vital.

One way to review your goals is to use SMART as a litmus test. Are they **S**pecific, **M**easurable, **A**chievable / **A**ctionable, **R**elevant, and **T**ime-bound? Do you want them to be? The very idea of making a goal match up to the SMART acronym puts some people off goal setting entirely.

*What's next?*
Keep reading, because we're going to explore what goals are and how to achieve them in more detail. Consider the reality check over (for a while at least)! I'll talk more about whether a goal needs to be SMART in the chapter in productivity. For now, let's turn to something much more amiable – the science of happiness.

# Chapter 6: The Science of Happiness

### About this chapter

Happiness is a hot topic. Some governments are using happiness measures in the same way that GDP is used, as an indication of standards of living. This chapter asks the question: is happiness the ultimate goal?

We begin by looking at a quick definition of happiness and several happiness pioneers – people who've influenced our understanding of happiness over the last few years. Then we'll examine different ways of measuring happiness, followed by a survey of different versions of happiness.

After that we'll puzzle out how other people are involved in our happiness, because it turns out that the amount of support you get *and* the amount of autonomy you have affect your reported happiness levels.

You'll also get some practical exercises to try and suggestions for small steps you can take to improve your own happiness and to build your support network.

### *A definition of happiness*

We're thinking about happiness in relation to goals setting, because the two go hand-in-hand. We can define happiness as follows. If your goals lead you to enhance or emphasise any of these, you'll also be boosting your happiness:

- Authenticity – living according to our values.
- Autonomy – having control over our own lives.
- Connections – forging deep connections with people (and animals).
- Enough-ness – feeling we are enough, and we have enough.
- Gratitude – regularly reminding ourselves what we're grateful for.
- Kindness – being able to give to others.

- Meaning – feeling we've contributed to something meaningful or bigger than ourselves.
- Play – having at least some time put aside to relearn our childlike joy, to be light-hearted, take breaks, be creative, rest and daydream.

## Happiness Pioneers

*Tara Brach*
Buddhist and meditation teacher, Dr Tara Brach, wrote the groundbreaking book *Radical Acceptance*. The central tenant being that we can't make progress or change unless we first accept reality as it is now. Tara Brach publishes free talks and meditations on her website.

*Brené Brown*
Professor, and vulnerability and shame researcher, Brené Brown became famous when her TED talk on the Power of Vulnerability went viral, and it has now gained over 60 million views. She hosts two podcasts and has written several books including *The Gifts of Imperfection* and *Daring Greatly*.

*Ed Diener*
A Professor of Psychology, Ed Diener was a leading researcher in the field of well-being, so much so he was nicknamed Dr Happiness. In 2006, he gave an interview with the BBC, where he talked about "having goals embedded in your long-term values that you're working for, but also that you find enjoyable." In 2008, he co-wrote *Happiness: Unlocking the Mysteries of Psychological Wealth* with his son Dr Robert Biswas-Diener, who has also written widely on Positive Psychology.

*Dan Harris*
Former ABC News Anchor, Dan Harris, started out as a meditation sceptic and now writes about and trains people in meditation, aiming to make us '10% Happier' – hence the name of his meditation app and first book. The list of contributors to the app and podcast reads like a 'who's who' of North American meditation teachers – providing a wonderful

way of exploring the practice further, as many, such as Oren Jay Sofer and Sebene Selassie, have written books themselves.

*Russ Harris*
Dr Russ Harris, pioneer of acceptance and commitment therapy (or ACT) leads online courses and has written a bestselling book called *The Happiness Trap*, a toolbox that will help you to overcome anxiety and live more fully. ACT challenges us to live authentic lives based on our values.

*Dacher Keltner*
A Professor of Psychology, who hosts the Science of Happiness podcast, Keltner runs the Greater Good Science Center at the University of California at Berkeley. His books include *Born to Be Good: The Science of a Meaningful Life*.

*Kristin Neff*
Self-Compassion expert Dr Kristin Neff has written extensively about how learning to care for ourselves improves our physical and mental health. She leads courses for the public and for therapists and has written a self-help guide called *The Mindful Self-Compassion Workbook*.

*Laurie Santos*
One of the most interesting developments in happiness research in recent years has come out of Yale University. Prof Laurie Santos's *The Science of Well-Being* course – and the new version for teenagers – has been made available for free online and is well worth a look. Santos starts the course by telling students that she too is on a journey to find out what happiness means – and she invites us to come along with her for the ride.

*Martin Seligman*
Pioneer of Positive Psychology, which posits the idea that psychology shouldn't only be remedial (i.e., help people with problems) but can also be used to enhance our lives and make us authentically happier, hence the title of his book *Authentic Happiness*. According to Seligman,

the dimensions of happiness, which we can foster and develop, are "the Pleasant Life, the Good Life, and the Meaningful Life".

## Different happiness measures
*Gross National Happiness or GNH*
This is the concept, originating in Bhutan, that the happiness of a nation can be measured just as the Gross Domestic Product (GDP) can be measured. One proposal for testing GNH takes in:

- Economic wellness
- Environmental wellness
- Physical wellness
- Mental wellness
- Workplace wellness
- Social wellness
- Political wellness

*Your Better Life Index*
The Organisation for Economic Co-operation and Development (or OECD) has created a 'Better Life' index, which compares eleven areas that are key to people's wellbeing across different countries. The suggestion here is that i) society-wide factors affect our happiness levels ii) improving these eleven areas would increase people's happiness. The eleven topics compared by the OECD are:

- Community
- Education
- Environment
- Governance
- Health
- Housing
- Income
- Jobs
- Life Satisfaction
- Safety
- Work / Life Balance

*The Happiness Index*
In 2010, a survey, commissioned by the UK government, attempted to discover how happy we are in Britain. The Office for National Statistics (ONS) asked 200,000 people the following questions, which participants scored out of ten:

- How satisfied are you with your life nowadays?
- How happy did you feel yesterday?
- How anxious did you feel yesterday?
- To what extent do you feel the things you do in your life are worthwhile?

The ONS still collect this data. It's now known as the 'National Wellbeing Index.'

## Different kinds of happiness

*Happiness not positive thinking*
Happiness is not the same as positive thinking, something Oliver Burkeman writes about in *The Antidote: Happiness for People Who Can't Stand Positive Thinking*. Researchers have found that genuine happiness has much more to do with living authentically, in line with your values, and having autonomy, than it is about feeling positive all of the time.

*The comparison paradox*
We know that happiness is relative: reported happiness levels in surveys often depend on comparisons we make with those around us. However, deep happiness results from *loosening* the ties that bind our happiness to these comparisons, and *strengthening* the ties that connect us, genuinely, with other people.

*Can money buy happiness?*
Not having much money (or being worried about money) can make you very unhappy but financial security and happiness are not the same thing. Not everyone is motivated by money. Many people are motivated by friends, family or spirituality, for example. Conversely, striving for

## 6: THE SCIENCE OF HAPPINESS

financial security provides some people with motivation to work, which gives meaning to their lives. Winning the lottery would spell disaster for them. For these people, money is a motivation, just not a direct one. Some commentators argue that happiness results from being paid about the same amount as people you know, having a similar number of possessions, living in a comparative sized house. In other words, reported happiness is equated with both financial stability and comparability.

*Acquiring something we don't have*
It's possible to invest one particular thing we perceive as lacking from our lives with happiness. If only I had X, such as a stable relationship, a house, a round-the-world ticket, a job, a baby, I would be happier. This isn't just frippery – these things would have a real effect, although not necessarily positive – and it would be tempting to start craving the next thing I don't have after acquiring the original! The trouble with this way of thinking is that we miss the possibility for happiness now, and we miss out on enjoying and learning from the journey.

*A happy old age*
When some people talk about happiness, they are literally talking about a specific future in which they are able to 'retire happy'. Happiness to them means financial security, good health and good relationships into old age. From this point of view, it is worth making sacrifices now to achieve happiness. But what about being happy in the moment?

*Mindfulness*
Mindfulness means cultivating awareness and being present the moment. You don't have to be Buddhist to benefit from mindfulness. According to this idea, it's dangerous to assume that we will reach a happy point somewhere in some vague future once all our goals are achieved.

To many people, the word 'pursuit' in 'the pursuit of happiness' is misleading, even debilitating. We don't have to pursue anything. Each moment is enough just as it is. Tara Brach explains this concept further *Radical Acceptance*, as does Eckhart Tolle in *The Power of Now*.

*Is happiness the hidden goal behind all other goals?*
Is 'I want to be happy' the ultimate hidden goal behind all of our goals? If all of your goals *don't* ultimately lead to happiness – which, according to the happiness pioneers, isn't the same as instant pleasure or freedom from challenges – is there any sense in pursuing them? That said, setting goals that align with your values is one way to make sure that you are doing what you want to be doing in life – you don't yet know if they will somehow 'make you happy' in the future.

*What can you do about it?*
If you've followed the suggestions so far in this book and you've been honest about setting goals, you've already taken steps towards creating a happy life, now and in the future. Here are some other suggestions:

- Read some of the happiness literature listed in the resources section or look into the Yale course mentioned above.
- Find out about mindfulness. I like Tara Brach's free meditations and I also use the 10% Happier App.
- Decide how much you are equating happiness with i) financial security; ii) some point in the future – either vague or specific; iii) pleasure; iv) something you don't have.
- Check your goals are aligned with your values.

## Making other people happy
*Feel like a doormat?*
'I've spent my life making other people happy'. This idea is often used as a negative, as if we can't become happy at the same time. What's wrong with making other people happy? In fact, making other people happy is genuinely happiness-creating, as long as the relationship is reciprocal – you get a lot out of it too. If you've spent your life making other people happy, congratulate yourself – it's a wonderful thing to do. If what you really mean is 'I've spent my life being a doormat' or 'I'm taken for granted', here are some suggestions:

- Have another look at the exercise on 'the story of your success'. The problem might be that you need to reframe how you think about the world.
- Do one thing today that is just for you and no one else, even if it's simply having a bath or going for a walk or sitting down to read a magazine. Do something just for you every day from now on and keep a note of it in your journal.
- We often underestimate the importance of healthy eating and exercise on our mental health. This is part of looking after yourself. Take a small step today: make a healthy meal for yourself or go swimming at your local pool, for example.
- Make a list of things you are grateful for and people you appreciate as often as possible. Do it before you go to bed or on your journey to work or on a walk round the block. People I do this gratitude exercise with are usually surprised at how long their list grows once they give themselves permission to fill the page.

*Happy teams*
Selfish individuals perform better than altruistic individuals, but altruistic groups perform better than selfish groups. This is taken from evolutionary biology, but I'm going to borrow it and change the meaning (with unreserved apologies to all evolutionary biologists), as follows: if you work in a group where everyone behaves altruistically towards one another, that group will out-perform groups of people who are behaving selfishly towards one another.

This is most relevant, in our context, to families and to teams who need to work together.

*Practical suggestions for building altruistic groups*
The difficulty here is to build an environment where people are *able* to act altruistically towards one another and where they trust each other enough to do so. People's *total* need has to be considered and their *total* skillset taken into consideration: not just those needs and skills that they regularly bring to the group. This will take training and can't be solved

using a quick fix – one day spent doing trust building exercises won't achieve very much. I suggest starting by:

- Being honest and direct about the aims of the group.
- Having regular check ins, that allow everyone to be heard.
- Making sure everyone has somewhere to put their things (somewhere they belong).
- Allowing everyone in the group to have input into the way rewards and sanctions are administered. Reward reciprocal skill-sharing behaviour or anything the group defines as 'non-selfish'.

## Support from others, supporting others

*Direct and indirect support*
There are two kinds of support when it comes to goal setting: direct support, for example, attending an NHS Stop Smoking group, and indirect support, for example, the support we might get from friends and family when quitting smoking. Sometimes just having someone to hang out with is enough. We don't have to tell everybody and anybody about our goals.

*Dependence and autonomy?*
We know that researchers have discovered that both social relationships *and* the amount of autonomy you have affect your happiness. In addition, research has shown that it is easier to achieve specific goals if we get some support. In other words, it's important that we can make choices and have control over our lives; it's also important that we depend on others. You can treasure your own autonomy *and* build direct and indirect support for your goals. How? By being proactive while taking small steps.

*Support for my goal*
Stop and try this exercise now. Take one of your goals. Create a spider diagram in your journal showing the support you will need to achieve your goal. Write the goal in the middle of the page. Put a circle around it. Who are you relying on for help? Add more circles with names then connect them to your goal. For example, if you need a loan to start a

business, that's direct support: add the bank's small business advisor to your diagram. Add people who offer indirect support. For example, if your parents look after your children once a week, and indirectly support your goal, they go onto the diagram.

Do you know about the dreams, ambitions, hopes and fears of any of the people on your diagram? Probably only if they are close friends or family members or if you know the career aims of any colleagues on your list. Do you notice any opportunities to create a reciprocal relationship, where you can offer support in return? Do you notice any clashes between their goals and yours? For example, if you rely on your parents for childcare once a week, that would interfere with their ambition to sail around the world.

*Interdependence v. Independence*
In a sense, everyone is dependent: it is almost impossible to achieve our goals independently. We need support from other people, directly and indirectly. We need to work with and trust other people. That's a good thing. It makes the journey more rewarding. We can, however, be independent in the sense that we're individually responsible for our actions and reactions and for planning our lives. That's also a good thing.

For example, when trying to achieve a goal to exercise more when our son was still a baby, it was a huge help when I found a really good teacher. By really good, I don't mean good at sport, though I imagine she is that too. I mean a really good *teacher*. I wasn't friends with her; I hardly even spoke to her, but she was inspiring and motivating and crucially for me she provided me with the right support at the right time.

*Supporting others*
For a holistic approach, caring for the people who are close to us, and knowing about their dreams as well as their more everyday goals, must be part of any goal you take on. No goal will lead to happiness without this aspect. It's a part of the process that many goal setting techniques ignore. It is crucial not only to have the support of people around you, but to support them in return.

GOAL SETTING AND TIME MANAGEMENT

*Co-dependence*
Co-dependence – a word much used by therapists – is when we don't take responsibility for ourselves. If you've got this far through the book and you've been working through the exercises, you've gone a long way towards taking responsibility for your future, but if you think your relationships with others are getting in the way of your happiness, there are plenty of small steps suggested in this chapter to help you. You might also want to seek help from a counsellor.

*The importance of friendship*
Don't underestimate the importance of having friends around you. Loneliness makes you unhappy. It can become a vicious circle. The lonelier we feel, the more withdrawn we can become. Loneliness can distort your sense of what's important in life, so that it's hard to work out what your goals are, and it can also stop you from achieving them. The flipside can also be true. Stopping at nothing to achieve our goals might lead to loneliness. If any of this strikes a chord with you, take some of the small steps listed below.

*How to find direct support:*
- Take a small step today: if it's relevant, find out about a support group you can join to help you achieve your goal. For direct support, the activity of the group will be related to your goal somehow.
- For a health or career-related goal there are likely to be formal groups advertising online, at work, in the local library, in your GP's Surgery, or community centre, or at the Citizen's Advice Bureau. Look out for social prescribing in your local area.
- Think creatively. For example, if your goal is to find a life partner, joining a book group or a wine tasting club or forming a pub quiz team or training as a football coach may mean you meet like-minded people.
- Some direct support will be one-on-one: with a nutritionist, a careers advisor or a fitness instructor, for example. One-to-one

support doesn't have to be expensive. Some people qualify for support through the NHS.
- Return to the list of skills you wrote in the very first chapter during the activity suggested under '*Do you need a goal?*' Could you swap skills with someone? Volunteering can also be a creative way to tap into direct support.

*How to build a wider support network:*
- If you need help building a support network, try this. You need a blank sheet of paper. Draw a diagram with yourself in the middle. At the top write "my support network". Add anyone you consider part of your wider support network, whether you are related or not. Take your time.
- Grateful list time again! Spend some time writing a grateful list specifically about the people in your life. What do you appreciate most about the people around you?
- Organise social events for your existing friends.
- Sometimes we need to build new friendships deliberately. Again, return to the list of skills you wrote. Could you develop any of these as a way of making contact with people? Could you volunteer somewhere?
- Either take an interest you already have and research ways of meeting people through it or find a new interest and join a group that welcomes beginners.
- Pick an established group that organises social events as well as their regular sessions, Zoom meetups, rehearsals or training. For example, a sports team, a choir, a meditation group, or a performing arts group.

*Goal check: what does happiness look like?*
It may be obvious how your goals fit with your overall happiness levels, but if not, try these exercises:
- Your happiness picture. With your eyes closed, visualise what happiness looks like, specifically, for you.

GOAL SETTING AND TIME MANAGEMENT

- What will it take for you to be happy now, in one week, one month, one year, five years and in ten years? Again, visualise what happiness looks like.
- Your partner's happiness picture. Ask your partner or the person closest to you to repeat this exercise so you can compare results.
- Goal check. Now look back at the goals you've written down. Do your goals fit your happiness picture? Are any getting in the way?

*What's next?*

Take a look at the Very Well Mind website, where you'll find an article that neatly sums up what sciences knows about being happy. https://www.verywellmind.com/what-is-happiness-4869755

In the next chapter, I'm going to review different goal setting methods, as well as several books that discuss how to focus and avoid distraction.

# Chapter 7: A Review of Goal Setting Methods, Including the Goal-Free Method

### About this chapter
In this chapter I've taken some of the most popular goal setting resources around and have divided them into categories according to their themes and ideas. These categories are my invention and are somewhat artificial as there is some overlap, but the intention is to show you what's out there. In other words, I've done some of the hard work for you, so you don't have to search too far for the materials that are right for you. The categories are:

- Productivity, work or sales goals
- The habits of success
- Focus / avoiding distraction
- Using life roles or the whole self
- Channelling mistakes and perseverance
- Being journey-focused

You'll find details on all of the books and resources mentioned in the final section of this book. Because the methods reviewed here involve motivating people to succeed, many of them come in different formats: websites, motivational talks, workshops, audio book format, YouTube videos, online courses, as well as books.

These reviews contain my subjective opinion. There's no substitute for trying any appealing ideas out for yourself but you certainly don't need to read / watch all of them in order to succeed at goal setting. Find methods that you like, which might take a bit of trial and error, and practise. Beware of anything offering results in 24 hours!

## Productivity, work or sales goals

*Summary*

These goal setting methods tend to be focused on motivation in the workplace. Occupying this category, are books and programmes for managers who want to motivate their employees as well as books for individuals who want to find a job they love. The ideas are often related to jobs that involve selling. These are the goal setting methods that you might see satirised in film comedies, but that doesn't mean that none of the techniques will work for you.

At their worst they can be focused on a very narrow definition of 'success' and encourage adherents to stop at nothing to get sales. This means they sometimes don't consider the whole person and the techniques suggested can therefore feel rather flimsy.

At their best, they help people to become more assertive in a work situation and to find work that motivates them. One could argue – as Daniel H. Pink does – that everyone needs to be able to 'sell' something, at least in its broadest sense: a teacher convincing a parent to read to his children is selling the idea that reading is important, a neighbourhood campaign to raise money for a community centre has to sell the idea to supporters. One could also argue that because almost everyone works (though not necessarily in paid work or in sales, something these types of resources tend to forget) any well-written guide to getting the most out of your working life is potentially useful.

*Brian Tracy*

Brian Tracy is a management consultant, bestselling author and motivational speaker. His books aren't subtle. *Goals!* is emblazed in large letters across the cover of the book with that title and has the tagline *Get Everything You Want – Faster Than You Ever Dreamed,* and I couldn't avoid feeling that I was being shouted at when I read it. I was left feeling that it might be better, after all, to get some of what you want slowly or not to get everything you want but to enjoy the journey!

*Goals!* does contain useful advice and practical exercises. For example, Tracy's "seven keys to goal setting" can be usefully applied to any goal.

## 7: A REVIEW OF GOAL SETTING METHODS

According to chapter six, you need to make goals "specific", "measurable", time limited, "challenging", value-bound and "balanced", a lot like SMART goals. Plus, all of your goals should move you towards an overarching life goal. That's all very well, as long as it's possible to add 'desirable' or even 'enjoyable' to the mix!

*Eat That Frog: 21 Great Ways To Stop Procrastinating and Get More Done In Less Time* is probably Tracy's most famous book. The 'frog' refers to today's most challenging task and how we should 'eat that frog' first.

*Who else writes about it?*
- Zig Ziglar was a motivational speaker and author, who spoke about selling and work-related performance.
- Spencer Johnson was another bestselling author, who wrote *Who Moved My Cheese?*, about managing change at work.
- Daniel H. Pink's *To Sell is Human* is an interesting take on selling and how we all have to do it.
- Michael Hyatt's *Your Best Year Ever* takes you through a series of powerful mindset and goal setting techniques. His take on SMARTER goal setting is included in the book.
- I also like *Start With Why* by Simon Sinek, who invites us to drill down into our purpose or our 'why' before taking action.

Related to this category are books that come with a dose of non-conformity, by a new generation of entrepreneurs, such as *The 4-Hour Workweek* by Tim Ferriss, Chris Gullibeau's *The Art of Non-Conformity*, *$100 Start Up* and *Side-Hustle*, and *Chillpreneur* by Denise Duffield-Thomas, all of which were inspired by world travel.

## The habits of success
*Summary*
Typified by the famous, bestselling *Seven Habits of Highly Effective People*, this approach tends to look at how successful people have achieved their goals in the past and breaks down the approach into traits, rules or habits for others to follow. Malcolm Gladwell's *Outliers* could also fit into this

category as it details the routes to success taken by some of the world's most successful people, from Bill Gates to The Beatles.

*Stephen Covey*
Covey's work is so influential that many other goal setting or self-help books owe a debt to him. Habit one, "be proactive" surely underpins the adoption of almost any method or technique: as I like to say to my students, you can't get published / get a job / research an essay whilst sitting on the sofa eating crisps. Habit four: "think win / win" has entered popular culture as a self-help idiom.

As per the title, Covey unpacks seven habits that he has identified in successful people across a spectrum of disciplines and walks of life. Simply knowing the chapter headings and what they mean will provide some useful advice when setting goals! For example, habit seven "sharpen the saw" involves making sure you take care of yourself. Covey divides "you" into the following life parts, a coaching technique we're already familiar with. He uses: "physical", "mental", "spiritual" and "social / emotional", and argues that we must recharge and renew each aspect of ourselves.

*Who else writes about it?*
- Robert Kelsey in *What's Stopping You?* Kelsey describes how to develop strategies to deal with what he calls "high fear of failure". Part two is about goals. Kelsey includes mention of several self-help and popular psychology books.
- Mason Currey's successful blog 'Daily Routines' has spawned two books. *Daily Rituals* and the follow up, *Daily Rituals: Women at Work*, which outline the routines of creative people, in fascinating detail.
- Each chapter of *Metamorphosis: How and Why We Change* by Polly Morland discusses a different person who has radically changed their life.

Related to this category are books that don't so much show us how successful people did it, but encourage us to build healthy habits ourselves, so we're much more likely to achieve our goals. One theme that links

## 7: A REVIEW OF GOAL SETTING METHODS

these books is that they are often about change. Those I've enjoyed that encourage habit forming include:

- *Atomic Habits* by James Clear
- *The Power of Habit* by Charles Duhigg
- *How to Change* by Katy Milkman
- *The Courage Habit* by Kate Swoboda

## Focus / avoiding distraction

*Summary*

These approaches don't set out to tell you how to set goals in the first place – they're about how to avoid distraction in trying to achieve them. Symptomatic of a modern world with seemingly endless distractions – including one most of us carry around with us everywhere (i.e., our phones!) – these resources offer ways to fight back.

Books in this category tend to be practical. They give you different strategies to use to sharpen your focus or to combat distraction. Therefore, it's going to help if you focus on a particular goal as you go. You'll also want to implement the strategies as you read, or make notes that are easy to access (use colour coding or underlining / circling / annotations) otherwise it will be difficult to remember the suggestions once you've read the book. Ironically, it's easy to get distracted by the next new focusing technique and forget to implement the ones we've already learnt!

*Cal Newport*

*Deep Work* by Cal Newport, a Georgetown University professor, is a detailed and interesting discussion about our ability to focus – claiming that those who are able to go deep into whatever they are working on have a massive advantage. Newport followed up with a book called *Digital Minimalism*, arguing we should radically cut back on our use of (and therefore on the influence of) social media, smart phones, and the online world generally.

I found *Deep Work* to be an extremely useful thinking tool – a book that challenged me to find more thoroughly distraction-free time to focus for sustained periods on what really matters to me. It's less of a techniques-based book than the others I mention here – more of a treatise on why we need to work deeply, and the benefits of doing so. The cynical part of me did wonder about the circumstances that had allowed Newport to write the book in the first place, circumstances that aren't available to all of us.

*Who else writes about it?*
- Neuroscientist Daniel Levitin's *The Organised Mind* uses developments in brain science to show you how to overcome distraction.
- *Free to Focus* by Michael Hyatt accompanies a range of planners and journals – which I have personally found useful – with associated online training packages.
- *Indistractable* by Nir Eyal, is a techniques-focused book that has become an online course, and one of those you need to implement while you read it to remember the strategies involved.
- In *How to Focus* by Thich Nhat Hanh, the late Buddhist monk and inspirational meditation teacher lays out the foundations of mindfulness.
- Johann Hari's *Stolen Focus* is the result of three years of research into our shortening attention spans.
- Buffett talks about focusing on a maximum of 5 goals, Gary Keller suggests just one, in his book *The One Thing*.
- *The Disorganized Mind* by Nancy Ratey is full of practical strategies that helped me improve my executive functioning skills.

## Using life roles or the whole self
*Summary*
This kind of goal setting method involves breaking your life into categories. When using the Wheel of Life, typically, a coach would invite coachees to decide how satisfied they are in each area and to rate it out of ten. Some writers give broad categories and I've already mentioned Covey's above.

Instead of using the general categories of the Wheel of Life, you

## 7: A REVIEW OF GOAL SETTING METHODS

might be encouraged to create your own bespoke list of roles such as parent, daughter, business owner etc. – as you did in chapter three. This more personal approach allows you to prioritise the roles that are most important to you.

Breaking our lives down like this allows us to do two things:

1) After working out which areas are important to us, we'll know whether we're achieving balance across the different parts of our lives.
2) We can identify goals for each category or role.

*What's wrong with this approach?*
There are a few problems with this way of doing things. The most obvious one is that all of the areas of our lives intersect, and we can't necessarily think about one part of our lives without involving several others. The second is that because most of us play lots of different roles at home and at work, we can easily end up with too many goals. Also, what about goals that are not related to any of your current roles or categories? I might secretly want to be a jazz pianist, but if I've never opened the lid of a piano and don't listen to any jazz, it might not appear on my list of roles or categories. That said, the books I have read of this type tend to acknowledge these problems.

*Jinny Ditzler*
When I first read Ditzler's *Your Best Year Yet* in my twenties, I found it epiphanic. It was the first time I had consciously thought about setting goals based on an audit of where I was and where I wanted to go. As a result of implementing the strategies in Ditzler's book, I got onto a leading MA programme in Creative Writing, won a sort-after bursary, and published two novels.

Broken down into ten questions, each one involving practical exercises, Ditzler shows you how to make your next year the 'best year yet' hence the title of her book. When I've led workshops on Creative Careers for MA students, I've recommended the book, and now some of the participants also use Ditzler's questions every year. Questions six, seven and eight give you practical exercises for achieving balance across different areas of your life.

*Who else writes about it?*
- Life coach Martha Beck has written several books including *Finding Your Way In A Wild New World*.
- Life coach and NLP practitioner Kate Burton structures her book *Live Life, Love Work* around physical, mental, emotional and purposeful energy.
- Leading life coach Brooke Castillo's *Self-Coaching 101* helped me with the crucial mindset aspects of goal setting. She also has a podcast.
- There is a section on goal setting in *The Mind Map Book* by Tony Buzan, great if you like drawing or visualisations. *The Mind Map Book* doesn't focus on life roles, but one way to identify your goals is to mind map your life roles, which is why I've included it here.
- In his practical book about creating a life plan, *Living Forward*, Michael Hyatt suggests we use life roles to create a balanced set of goals in different areas of our lives.
- Brian Mayne's *Goal Mapping* incorporates thinking on the law of attraction and positive thinking. I've put him in this category because if you follow his exercises and draw your goal map you'll break your life into parts and take small steps back from your main goal. If you like this book, you may also like *The Book of Afformations* by Noah St. John.

## Channelling mistakes and perseverance
*Summary*
This is the idea that one doesn't need inborn talent to succeed, but rather constant practice. Making mistakes, failing, examining where we went wrong and trying again are good things and should be cultivated as an approach rather than avoided – in fact doing so is the only way to change. Carol Dweck's *Mindset* championed the idea of learning from (so-called) failure in order to grow and can be thought as the founder

member of this category. The importance of perseverance rather than innate talent came to particular prominence after the publication of Malcolm Gladwell's *Outliers*.

*10,000 hours and beyond*
Based on research by the late psychologist Anders Ericsson, the 10,000 hours 'rule' – that Malcolm Gladwell made famous – states that you need 10,000 hours or ten years to become a virtuoso violinist or, by extrapolation, to master a skill. In *Peak: How All of Us Can Achieve Extraordinary Things* by Anders Ericsson and Robert Pool, you'll get much more detail on Ericsson's research. The depth of approach in *Peak* makes the more well-known *Outliers* seem like a simple introduction to the idea. You'll find online articles 'debunking' the 10,000 hours 'rule' – better to get more depth by returning to the source of the research!

*Angela Duckworth*
Angela Duckworth, a psychologist and professor at UPenn, studied the meaning of success and wrote *Grit: Why Passion and Resilience are the Secrets to Success* about her research findings. *Grit* expands on Carol Dweck's foundational work on mindset. Finding your purpose – something you're passionate about – motivates you to keep going. Duckworth's PhD supervisor was Martin Seligman, founder of the Positive Psychology movement, and she now works with Katy Milkman – author of *How to Change* – at the Behavior Change for Good Initiative. Duckworth hosts a popular podcast called *No Stupid Questions*. She also gave one of the most viewed TED talks ever.

*What's wrong with this approach?*
- The 10,000 hours 'rule' appears to be the polar opposite of Brian Tracy's promise to bring you success "faster than you ever dreamed". In other words, knowing about it feels daunting. We have to begin somewhere, and sometimes the first year is just the beginning. If you have a big ambition, don't let 10,000 hours scare you. Start with one small thing.

- The main criticism of the 'grit' approach is that we also need to take into account socioeconomic and other wider factors of the kind mentioned by the happiness measures in Chapter 6. Suggesting that 'you simply need more determination' – which to be fair on Duckworth is a reductive way to sum up her findings – fails to acknowledge these contexts, that adversely affect people from disadvantaged backgrounds.

*Who else writes about it?*
- Tim Harford is the economist behind *The Undercover Economist*. In his follow up book *Adapt: Why Success Always Starts With Failure*, he describes how companies and individuals who try flexible and varied approaches – accepting failure as part of that approach – are most likely to find success. He's written several other books since, including *Messy: How to Be Creative and Resilient in a Tidy-Minded World*.
- In Matthew Syed's *Bounce: The Myth of Talent and the Power of Practice*, the table-tennis champion and sports journalist describes what he calls the "hidden logic of success", involving hard work and training rather than inborn talent. He's since written several other popular psychology books, including a couple of mindset workbooks for kids *You are Awesome* and *Dare to Be You*, bringing these ideas to a wider audience.

## Being journey-focused
*Summary*
Journey-focused philosophies encourage us to consider the process, to think about the present moment and to practise mindfulness. Usually the journey is an emotional, creative or spiritual one. This isn't so much a strategy for directly working on your goals, rather you figure things out slowly through journaling or through meditation practice or walking or travelling, for instance. Some writers in this category advocate living goal-free. The journey metaphor might seem to suggest that we're heading to a destination, whereas in fact in this approach it's the journey itself

## 7: A REVIEW OF GOAL SETTING METHODS

that matters, and not our arrival. In fact, one proponent of this sort of philosophy Alan Watts, talks about why 'life is not a journey,' precisely because, according to Watts, we're not going anywhere. These kinds of ideas provide a counterpoint to those that set us striving towards achieving bigger and better goals at some point in the future.

*Goal-free living*
Although it sounds like it from the title of Stephen M. Shapiro's book, *Goal-Free Living* isn't exactly anti-goals, but rather anti-blinkered stress-inducing goals. Shapiro talks about developing aspirations instead of ridged goal setting. Remember SMART goals from earlier? It's this kind of results-orientated goal setting Shapiro critiques in *Goal-Free Living*. His philosophy reminds me of Dweck's "growth mindset". Each encounter and challenge is an opportunity to learn something new.

Shapiro structures his book using the "eight secrets of goal-free living" which allows him to elaborate on these ideas. For example, secret one is "use a compass, not a map". This approach is very much about enjoying the journey but is the least spiritual of the books reviewed in this section. If you are a little concerned about the constraints of goal setting and targets then this will prove a useful book. However, if you are extremely suspicious of rigidly planned SMART-type goals, then Shapiro's book might not be radical enough for you!

*Who else writes about it?*
- Julia Cameron is a writer and artist who is most famous for creating *The Artist's Way* – 12-step programme for reclaiming our creativity – and has helped thousands of people. The practical techniques are useful for anyone who wants to follow a creative path. *The Sound of Paper,* about a journey, contains snippets of writing with practical suggestions at the end of each chapter. *Write for Life* will help with writing-related goals.
- Tara Brach. She's come up before, but now is a good point to say that the column Oliver Burkeman used to write in the *Guardian* called 'This Column Will Change Your Life' really did change my

life. Because of it, I read *Radical Acceptance* by Tara Brach. Through her meditations, website and books, Brach gives a unique take on applying mindfulness to everyday life. This is an inspirational book and a useful antidote to a life full of planning and struggling for success. Several of the motivational books I read when I started my research journey were recommended in Burkeman's column.
- Jack Kornfield. Another Buddhist teacher, Kornfield is a major influence on Tara Brach and his work is probably more about goal-free living than Shapiro's! He's written several books, including *After The Ecstasy, The Laundry* and *A Path with Heart*.
- Oliver Burkeman's *Help: How to Become Slightly Happier and Get a Bit More Done* gives snippets of down-to-earth advice about productivity and becoming happier (as the title suggests) and serves as a review of many different self-help books. However, in his more recent *Four Thousand Weeks* he confesses to being a recovering productivity addict and writes a treatise on why trying to reach happiness at some future point is futile – we should live our lives now.

## Commonalities and concluding thoughts
*Comparing the approaches*
We could place these books about goal setting and their attitude to it on a continuum. Brian Tracy's direct approach which leads to thorough planning, and very specific measurable, result-oriented goals would be at one end, with some of the other books about selling and performance at work, probably followed by the habits of success methods. The journey-focused writers would be at the other end: aspirations are encouraged, but here the approach is all about process, being OK now, being mindful of the present moment. What I've called 'using life roles or the whole self' and the 'channelling mistakes and perseverance' would feature somewhere in the middle. Having said that, one striking thing about these methods is that each has a structure, rules, guidelines, sometimes highly directed, sometimes merely suggested, but at the same time the *content* of the goals remains up to the reader.

## 7: A REVIEW OF GOAL SETTING METHODS

Instead of our continuum, we could let the differences between the approaches go into soft focus for a second and look at the wisdom we can glean from an overview:

- If you're going to have goals, specificity is a good idea.
- Knowing what your personal values are is crucial to all of these approaches.
- Whatever you do, don't be so focused on the results of your plan that you forget about either i) the process of getting there ii) being present in each moment.
- Making mistakes, facing challenges, and our attitude to failures are all crucial to achieving your goals.
- Effort is required. Instant results aren't a good thing.
- Thinking about the whole of your life and the different roles you play will stop you from becoming super-focused on one area to the detriment of others.

*What next?*
Personally, I've found Jinny Ditzler and Tara Brach inspiring so can highly recommend their work. That said, I hope I've given you enough information to decide for yourself whether you would like to follow up any of these leads. Next we're going to look at motivation – what it is, how to develop it, and whether you need it at all!

# Chapter 8: Motivation. What Is It? Do You Need It?

**About this chapter**
In this chapter, we start by trying to define motivation. Is it an abstract concept, an emotion, something busy people have, something other people have, or something everyone has? Next you're given some practical suggestions for developing more motivation, using the Small Steps Method. The rest of this chapter examines the different contradictions that arise when we try to pin down exactly what motivation is. I've given you lots of small steps exercises along the way so you can work out what motivation means to you.

**What is motivation?**
*An abstract concept*
The trouble with motivation is that it's an abstract concept. It's easy to imagine that motivation is a special force that exists either inside us or, elusively, 'out there' somewhere – or that it's an emotion that makes us feel ready to achieve whatever we want to achieve. When psychologists define it they tend to think of it as a desire to change. Once that desire becomes strong enough, that's motivation. What's more, our reasons for change need to be strong enough in the now – not far off in the future.

*So, is motivation an emotion?*
Equanimity comes from absence of guilt and tends to happen when we feel able to focus on one task at a time. It's possible to do absolutely nothing and feel fine. On the other hand, guilt or boredom are signs that you want or need to do something else, *not* that the task you're doing is uninteresting or unnecessary.

## 8: MOTIVATION. WHAT IS IT? DO YOU NEED IT?

According to Tara Brach, if you find yourself feeling bored or guilty, simply stopping, acknowledging and naming what you want or need to do can help.

Think of equanimity and guilt/boredom as two ends of a continuum. For some, motivation comes from being closer towards the equanimity end of this continuum and further away from the guilt or boredom end. For others, the very fact that they are not in a state of equanimity causes frustration – which creates just the friction they need to motivate them.

In other words, motivation isn't an emotion itself, but it has emotions attached to it.

*But aren't busy people more motivated?*
If you find that busyness is a motivating force, it's likely that, because you're busy, you've allocated the task a timeslot and that a side-effect of your busyness is at least partial efficiency. You're getting enough done to allow yourself to feel motivated.

If we think about it rationally, motivation is only a set of circumstances which, at the same time as providing us with the time and space to do whatever it is, and removing distractions, also make us feel committed and at ease. Given our busy lives, it's going to be a very happy coincidence if all of these circumstances and feelings happen at once.

*Does motivation come from other's expectations?*
This intriguing idea is explored in Gretchen Rubin's *The Four Tendencies*, which suggests that when it comes to expectations, we tend to react in particular predictable ways. We're either upholders, questioners, obligers, or rebels. According to the respondents of her survey, most people *are* motivated by the expectations of others, but a significant number aren't!

*Other people have it (or do they?)*
We might assume that everyone around us is motivated and feel demotivated ourselves. Fundamental attribution error is a term from psychology that is useful to apply here. It means that we assume, wrongly, that someone's behaviour is a result of an inner 'fundamental' trait. A

classmate is always late, we assume he or she is a late person. We're late, we blame it on our circumstances: the traffic was bad, the bus drivers were on strike. Arguably almost *every* action is a result of a particular set of circumstances or contexts rather than fundamental traits. When you see someone out jogging – looking motivated to keep fit – you don't know his or her circumstances. He or she is not necessarily or even probably 'fundamentally' motivated any more than you are. It follows that if we change our circumstances in just a small way – ask a friend to go jogging with us, join an NHS Stop Smoking Group – we don't need to be fundamentally motivated anyhow.

*Everybody has it (Why else do you get out of bed?)*
Thinking rationally again – which isn't easy to do when you're trying to muster up some motivation – everybody must have some kind of motivation. You're motivated enough to read these words. We're usually motivated enough to meet our basic physical needs. *Something* is making you do what you do all day, whether that's sitting on the sofa playing computer games and eating crisps, or going to work in a stressful job and coming home again. Far from being elusive, that motivational force is something we can harness.

By the way, if you ever find you have very little motivation at all, try taking a shower, fixing yourself some healthy food, taking care of yourself in any small way you can, and reaching out to someone for help.

*The Motivation Game: a day in the life*
Here's a small step you can take. Try playing the motivation game. Take one day in your life. Write down what you did. Make a list of all the key activities. Write down the reason you did each thing. We're not after deep reasons this time. Write down what made you do each activity in that particular moment in time. The motivation game proves that, somehow, we're already motivating ourselves. One thing that comes up again and again in the motivation game is habit. Why did you do X? *Because I always do X on a Monday afternoon.*

## How to develop more motivation

*Motivation and small steps*
Given that the 'reward' for our goals is often in the future, how on earth do you get motivated to achieve your goals? This is a conundrum that has filled many pages of self-help books. Motivation may not arrive until you start doing it. Following the methods in this book, take some small steps. Do these small, manageable steps daily and the motivation will follow. Here are some suggestions for making that work.

*Make it a habit*
We perform tasks habitually. This is a good thing. It would be a difficult life if we had to think carefully through the process of making a coffee or driving a car each time we did it. (You'll find books on habit formation listed in chapter 7.) Here's how to make the habit habit work for you:

- Focus on the time and the place when you'll do the thing (with flexibility) and on turning up there, because once you've started you're likely to keep going.
- Try to become more aware of your regular daily routines. Could you 'stack' new habits on existing ones – a technique James Clear calls 'habit stacking' in his book Atomic Habits? Or use accountability?
- Are you habitually doing anything that is sapping your motivation? For example, if your daily commute saps your energy: could you change the way you get to work or what you do on the way or could you work from home?
- In my book *Find Time to Write*, I discuss how to go about establishing a writing habit.

*Picture your higher motivations*
Higher motivations are the people and things that inspire you to achieve your goals, the people you love above anything else and the things you hold dear. For example, your children and your grandchildren or your desire to be fit into your old age or your commitment to caring for our planet.

## GOAL SETTING AND TIME MANAGEMENT

If you've been working through the exercises in this part of the book, you should know by now what you want to achieve. You know your smaller goals and you know your seemingly impossible dreams. Try this:

- Stop for a moment and review your goals, thinking about your motivations.
- Can you specifically name your higher motivations? For each one, keep asking 'why?' until you get to the underlying reasons.
- Tara Brach's meditation on communicating with your future self is available on YouTube. The link is in the resources section.

It's often when we come face-to-face with a specific example of a higher motivation that it becomes extremely powerful. This can be as simple as watching a grandchild playing on a beach. To go some way towards replicating this effect, keep a picture with you, a picture that reminds you of your higher motivations. It can be a physical picture or a detailed mental one. An object that reminds you of your higher motivations also works.

*Discover your values*
We've touched on values before, but here's a deeper dive. Most coaches, James Clear included, insist that you consider your values before working on your goals. Values infuse everything we do. They tend to be general guiding principles, rather than specific rules. Here are three ways to discover your values.

1. Your higher motivations will be underpinned by your values. Write down your higher motivation and work out the *belief* behind it. For example:

   | HIGHER MOTIVATION | VALUE |
   |---|---|
   | *I am motivated by…* | *I believe in…* |
   | My children and grandchildren | Parenting and family |
   | My desire to be fit into my old age | Health and wellbeing |
   | My commitment to caring for the planet | Environment and community |

2. Sometimes it's hard to know what your values are until they are challenged. Think about work-based or social scenarios that made you uncomfortable and ask yourself *why*.
3. Imagine the ideal you. How you are on your best days? How would you like other people to see you? Turn the ideal you into a list of single word descriptions. For example: funny, clever, witty, kind, loving, fair, good fun, laid-back. Put down as many as you can, then circle your top three. Based on your list, what are your values?

If you'd find it useful to take another look, go through the life roles you figured out in chapter three, and once you've jotted down what your values are, ask yourself if there any parts of your life where you are not living in line with these values.

*Solve your small wants*
Your higher motivations are probably different from your daily motivations. Jinny Ditzler talks about big and little wants in her book *Best Year Yet*. If you want to go to an exercise class regularly, your higher motivation – or 'big want' – may be the idea of living a fit and healthy life. When you wake up early on Monday morning, your 'small want' (an immediate want) might be to go back to sleep. The greater the disparity between your big wants and small wants, the more frustrated you'll feel. Sometimes the key to motivation is to *solve the small wants*. If I went to bed an hour earlier on Sunday night, perhaps I wouldn't want to go back to sleep quite so much on Monday morning. 'Small wants' might include:

- enough sleep
- a glass of water
- an adequate space to work
- encouragement and accountability from a partner or friend
- dealing with distractions and interruptions – have a look at some recommended books on focus in chapter 7 if this is a big deal for you.

*Your niggles list*
Write down every niggle in a list: anything that annoys you, interrupts you, frustrates you or prevents you from doing what you want to do, goal-related or otherwise. Spend some time recording these things in your journal. Solving these 'small wants' is an uplifting experience. You might find that you didn't need motivation, you needed to sort out the niggles.

*When small wants aren't so small*
A defining feature of 'small wants' is that they often go unidentified. When you begin to pin them down you might find they are part of a bigger problem – in other words they are not small at all. For example, 'enough sleep' features on the list of small wants above. Wanting to get back under the duvet instead of getting up to exercise doesn't seem so serious, but getting enough sleep is crucial for our health and vitality – are any of your small wants symptoms of a bigger problem? If so, have a go at working out some related small steps today, using the earlier chapters of this book.

*What motivates you to do what you do now?*
Review the results of the Motivation Game. You are already motivated to do these things. Can you simply change the activity – or most likely the habitual behaviour – to something more in line with your goals?

*Lack motivation? It's a sign!*
If you think you lack motivation, if you feel bored, guilty or frustrated, it's *a sign that something needs to change.* Reformulate your thinking and see your lack of motivation as a signal to do something different. Now you can take some action, just one small step. You might need to identify your 'small wants' and solve them first. Ironically you'll have used your apparent lack of motivation to kick start the process. The Small Steps Method is so effective because it focuses on taking one small step after another. Do one small thing towards changing your circumstances today.

## 8: MOTIVATION. WHAT IS IT? DO YOU NEED IT?

## You don't need motivation
*Do it anyway*
I first heard this advice from columnist Oliver Burkeman, who summed up psychologist's Julie Fast's work by saying "don't wait until you feel like doing something." Focus on the time and place you're going to do the thing, then turn up whether you feel like it or not.

*Have you tripped over a motivation stumbling block?*
You've tripped over a motivation stumbling block, if, as Oliver Burkeman points out, you wait until you feel motivated or inspired before doing something. This problem is something of a vicious circle: you'll end up getting stuck doing the same old thing, which makes it less likely you'll feel like it.

You may also have tripped over a motivation stumbling block if you start a task but don't see it through because you don't feel motivated. In this case, we typically feel enthusiastic about *starting* a project and excited about the *end result*, whether it's a weight-loss programme, or learning to speak Mandarin, but get frustrated by the *middle* of a project.

Of course, that's not the same as realising you're not fit enough, or that the activity is too dangerous, or that the goal isn't for you after all. Remember the alcoholic's prayer? This is when you need the 'wisdom to know the difference'. If you're part way through a project and feel like giving up, go back and review your goals in line with your values. If you're still in doubt, ask someone who knows you well whether you should keep going. And if you can find them, ask someone who's already done it for support.

If you don't feel motivated, do it anyway. Forget about what motivation is and how you develop it. You don't need it. Take one small step instead, and another and another. You can take small steps without motivation. As long as you are working on your goals, and you've thought them through in advance, how positive you feel about the individual steps doesn't matter. Just remember to make the steps small and specific.

GOAL SETTING AND TIME MANAGEMENT

*Turn up*
This is small steps principle number 8. Taking small steps means *turning up*. Applying it to writing, Julia Cameron calls this technique 'turning up at the page'. In other words, giving yourself the space and time to write, then sitting down to write and letting yourself off the hook. We turn up at the page, and then see what happens. You can apply the same idea to any goal you want to achieve. Give yourself adequate time and space to do it. Then turn up. Don't attempt to motivate yourself or analyse why you are there. If this is too difficult on your own, find a class to turn up to or turn up to your goal with a friend.

**Motivation doesn't exist!**
*Why we need structure (and confuse structure for motivation)*
It's possible that motivation doesn't really exist at all. It's just another word for structure, perseverance or habit. Take structure for instance. From your morning routine to the meeting schedule at work, to the train timetable on the way home, to the babysitting rota, we use structure to make sense of our day-to-day lives. Even if we think of ourselves as easy-going and flexible, we still have our own particular way of getting from breakfast to bedtime. What happens when we try to add something new? It disrupts the existing structure. We often confuse the unease this causes for lack of motivation.

We can also confuse the security we get from structuring our lives in a particular way with motivation. The (difficult) trick is to use the structure of our lives and build in time for the things we really want to achieve. By the way, this is why vague goals like 'I'll write my memoir one day' or 'I'll learn to scuba dive when I have some free time' don't work. Although as you saw in the previous chapter, Stephen M. Shapiro might not agree with me!

*Use routine and habit*
"Whatever you're meant to do, do it now. The conditions are always impossible." – Doris Lessing

Create a routine for the week and a routine for your day but make it flexible. Stick it up somewhere you can see it. What can you incorporate into your daily and weekly routine? Don't underestimate this tool: it replaces motivation with habit very quickly.

*Structure 101*
Structure isn't only about routine: our homes have a structure, our filing has a structure, our kitchen cupboards have a structure. Are the pans you need for cooking stuck on a shelf somewhere hard to reach? You may not have thought about it, you just curse to yourself every time you reach for the pans: but you are much more likely to be motivated to cook healthy meals instead of buying microwave dinners if those pans are within easy reach. You might actually be putting on weight because your pans are in an awkward cupboard! Make the structures in your life work for you.

*Incorporate and swap*
We know that habit is a key motivator in what we do already on a day-to-day basis. Where do you have space to incorporate a key goal-related activity? Which activities could you swap for something else to make them more goal-oriented? Try the kettle test if you need help to find time for a particular activity. I write about it on my website in relation to writing habits – but it can work for any goal. The link is in the resources section.

*The tyranny of 'instant results'*
Certain parts of modern culture encourage us to expect instant results. Internet search engines, instant celebrities created by reality shows, skin care products that are supposed to work in just a few seconds, diets that claim to get you slim in a week, lotteries that promise millions in prize money instantly. It's possible to become so tuned into the expectation of instant gratification that we associate it with the value and the quality of an experience or achievement.

*Listen to the masters*
Anyone who has become a master of a discipline – a master craftsman, an accomplished musician, bestselling author, a sculptor with many

years' experience, an Olympic athlete, a scientist or a medical pioneer who has spent many hours in training – will tell you that the reverse is true. Value and quality come from spending many hours, days, weeks and years perfecting and practising a skill. It's not only the end result that these masters of their craft, trade or science value. Listen to one of them being interviewed and more likely than not they'll say that although it was hard, and involved sacrifices, the process was as important as the end result. We're all familiar with this idea because we've all spent many hours, days, weeks and years perfecting and practising particular skills. These are often the ordinary everyday skills that we don't think twice about.

*Mistakes / practice / repetition*
We've talked about how humans learn by making mistakes. We make a mistake, practise and repeat. We're hardwired to learn like this because of the way human beings evolved to use tools and to communicate with one another. The expectation of instant gratification can exacerbate any motivation stumbling block and make us lose enthusiasm for a project as soon as it seems hard.

The trouble is, many people feel like giving up after the first mistake. We feel deflated. We lose enthusiasm. But we can't succeed unless we make mistakes. Therefore, your attitude to the process of mistakes / practice / repetition could govern your ability to succeed. We've already said that successful people have a different attitude to failure from everyone else. They see each knockback as a lesson. They deliberately set things in motion knowing that some approaches will fail but at least one will succeed.

This is why small steps principles 6 and 7 are so important. Do them and your attitude and motivation levels don't matter so much. Remember:

- Small steps don't necessarily go in a straight line.
- Take lots of small steps, especially at the beginning.

*Mistakes / practice / repetition exercise:*
This exercise is designed to get you thinking about how one masters a skill.

# 8: MOTIVATION. WHAT IS IT? DO YOU NEED IT?

1. Take one of the skills you identified in the first chapter under *'Do you need a goal?'* Something you can do well. Something you've known how to do for a long time. Write down how you acquired the skill.
2. Go out and learn something new. Take a day or a couple of evenings to learn the beginnings of it. Ideally ask someone who is already an expert to teach you the skill. Write down how you acquired the skill.
3. Teach someone a skill. Write down how they acquired the skill.

## Key motivation blind-spots

*Introducing the common motivation blind-spots*

Here are common goals that are notorious for motivation stumbling blocks. We tend to assume that we need to get motivated *before* we do each of these things while at the same time doing them or not doing them could have a major influence on our lives. The small steps suggested here are just that: suggestions. If these happen to be your personal goals, then go through the goal setting process outlined in the opening chapters of the book. All of these small steps demonstrate another crucial part of the Small Steps Method, summed up by principle number 4. After you've taken one small step, take another small step *even if the first step leaves you feeling demotivated, defeated or down-in-the-dumps*. Remember that when you plan your small steps they need to be as specific as possible.

*Quit smoking*

Don't wait for the will power. Take a small step. For example, stop by the health centre on the way to the shops to get a leaflet for a Stop Smoking group, get a book from the library on the way home from work, or make an appointment to see your doctor. Now plan your next small step.

*Exercise regularly*

Don't wait until you feel like it. Take a small step. For example, go for a swim instead of watching TV. Walk to work tomorrow morning. Do some gardening this weekend. Now plan your next small step.

*Eat healthily*
Take a small step. This evening, look online for an article or a recipe book that explains how foods affect your moods. Now plan your next small step.

*Creative activities*
There's something about dancing, singing, painting, writing, or expressing yourself creatively that makes you think and feel in a different way. Try it now. Put your favourite music on and move around the room to it. Or sing your favourite song as loud as you dare. Again, waiting for inspiration is a misnomer. Inspiration comes from doing it. Take a small step. For example, put aside one hour this week to do something creative that you've always wanted to try. Know nothing about it? Remember how we added the word 'research' earlier to create small steps? You could put aside one hour this week to research whatever it is and to create some small steps for yourself.

*I've always wanted to…(really?)*
We've talked about this before but it's worth revisiting. Sometimes we hold on to ambitions that don't really fit any more. Look again at the goals you've set for yourself, the skills you've identified and the values you hold. Is this goal – the thing you've always wanted to do – really worth holding onto? Why haven't you ever done it? Try to get down to the specific reasons. Take a small step. Do one thing this week towards realising this ambition. Or if it no longer suits you, let it go. Now plan your next small step.

## No need to get motivated
*Five practical exercises to help you get over a motivation stumbling block:*
- Your habits: over a week write down what you do habitually.
- Your key times: over a week write down your key stress points and record moments when you had time spare.
- Your small irritations: over a week record any small things that annoy you. Try go get down as many niggles as possible.

## 8: MOTIVATION. WHAT IS IT? DO YOU NEED IT?

- Your space: take a weekend (or longer of you need it) to make sure the space you live and work in is as easy to use as possible.
- Your stuff: take a weekend (or longer of you need it) to make sure the stuff around you is not only consummate with your values, but also isn't holding you back. The stuff around you needs to support you.

*What next?*
Now we're considered whether your goals are supposed to make you happy, and looked at the thorny issue of motivation, we've come to the end of the section on goal setting. In the second part of the book, we look at how to fit the small steps you've created into your routine, so keep that list handy as you read through the suggestions.

# PART 2
# TIME MANAGEMENT

# Chapter 9: Small Steps to Time Management

### About this chapter
This chapter introduces the second section of the book, which is all about small steps time management. I start by telling you more about what's included. Then I'll ask you to begin to think about time management and what it means. The chapter finishes with another look at the 10 principles of the Small Steps Method with an indication of how they apply to this section, plus a quick review of some popular time management methods. It's worth emphasising that in this section you should pick only the exercises you feel are relevant to your situation and that some are repeated and developed to help you practise particular techniques.

### Small steps time management: an introduction
*Included in this section:*
As I said, this section sets out the small steps approach to time management. When applying the ideas you'll find here, work with the goals you set in the previous section.

- We'll discuss productivity, how it's different from time management, and why, and whether you need it.
- We'll look at some examples of small steps time management in action and discover some time management basics and some tips for getting more specific.
- You'll analyse the way you use time, looking at your current rhythms and the peaks and troughs of your year.
- Then we'll go on to the core of small steps time management.
- Finally, we'll look at some small adjustments you can incorporate and small tools you can use to make time work for your goals.

## 9: SMALL STEPS TO TIME MANAGEMENT

*What is time management?*
The term 'time management' suggests that we can organise and control the way we use time. If you're interested in it, then there must be some periods of time in your life that you want to organise better. Time management is also big business with plenty of self-help books and business resources available on the subject. The term 'time management' also suggests that there's need for some kind of solution and that if only we could find out what it is, our organisational problems would be over! But no time management system can offer a magic wand. In order to introduce something new into our lives, we've either got to become more efficient or more organised (which isn't always possible) or stop doing something else, or all three. The good news is that in order to achieve your goals you *don't* have to schedule every minute of every day! There are some small and easy steps you can take to become more organised.

*Three things time management fundamentals*
1. We can't actually control or manage time, so think of time management as a catch-all for organisational strategies that help us get things done.
2. You can't forget your context when you're thinking about time management. Your context – the environment, people, spaces, resources and things that surround you – will either help or hinder you in the task you've set yourself. In turn, allowing for your context means you'll organise things more effectively.
3. Some things take time. Forget about instant results. To watch this in action, take a small step today and *plant something*. Go to a garden shop or call on a gardening friend. Put some bulbs down. Plant some seedlings. Get some herbs for your windowsill or a pot plant or think big – plant a tree. More on this below under 'garden time'.

*Why is time management important when you're setting goals?*
Without time management:
- goals become aspirational things, dreams that we want to achieve one day, things that we hope will happen by chance.

## GOAL SETTING AND TIME MANAGEMENT

- we may not be sure how long it will take us to achieve our goals or where the end point lies.
- we might know what the steps are – and even try multiple small steps to get us started – but we never make progress.
- we don't necessarily know whether we want to achieve our goals. Ironically, it's not until they stop being dreams and we make them part of our routine that we find out whether we really want to write a novel, say, or run a marathon.
- we won't know what it will cost us. We won't know what the commitment means.

*Turning up (again)*
To me this is a fundamental aspect of successful time management and one which is often ignored by self-help books. Earlier, I mentioned a student who was trying to write to the sound of her neighbours renovating their house. She thought she had writer's block. Her immediate problem was that she needed to find somewhere quiet to write, but when we delved a little deeper the issue was actually about turning up – small steps principle number 8. And turning up requires two things: *space and time*.

I've touched on this before, but I want to emphasise that turning up requires space, and *appropriate space* at that. My student needed somewhere peaceful to write. As we've discovered, we need somewhere *to turn up to* and we also need the right equipment.

Stop now and identify a problem you have related to organising your life or achieving your goals. Could it be solved by *turning up*? Do you need to work on time or space or both?

*Garden time*
Turning up requires time. Yes, we need a block of time when we are not required to do anything else, but also we need time in the way a garden needs time. You need to tend and care for a garden over years in order to take pleasure in seeing it grow and mature. Apply this to other tasks and projects in our lives and we could call it 'garden time'. My student needed to take the time to write one page and then another page and

## 9: SMALL STEPS TO TIME MANAGEMENT

then another, not just because the actual process of writing a book takes a block of time to accomplish, but because the project needed to mature and grow.

Remember what we said earlier about instant gratification? It can play havoc with time management. It can stop us doing anything that will require garden time. They say the best time to plant a tree was 25 years ago and the second best time is now.

So, now's the time to start digging! When you're creating a garden from scratch it helps to come up with some small steps and not to be overawed by the hugeness of the project. What's more, once you've created your plan, you're going to have to get down and dig at some point.

In a way, the student who thought she had writer's block didn't have a problem at all. She needed find an appropriate space and *to give it time*. She wasn't going to be able to write a novel in a week. Ironically we can get so hung up (often subconsciously) on the issue of substantial time commitment, that we don't do anything at all. If we take it seriously, the Small Steps Method solves this issue. Turn up, write a page. Turn up in front of YouTube, do the exercise. Turn up, buy some fresh vegetables. Whatever it is, take small steps and give it some garden time. Once you've realised this, you can let go of the amount of time it will take, and simply turn up regularly.

*The 10 small steps principles revisited*

Below I've repeated the 10 small steps principles, and I've pointed out in italics how you can use them to get to grips with time management. The rest of this section expands on these themes, showing you how to use it to achieve your goals.

1. Small steps are small. Break down a task until you get to something you could easily achieve today. *Once you've broken down a task like this, you can add the steps to your schedule.*
2. Small steps are specific and concrete. Make the small steps as down-to-earth and measurable as possible. *You can give yourself short deadlines. You'll know when you've completed the first steps.*
3. Small steps don't cost a fortune. Do as many free steps as possible

first. Financing a project can also be broken down into small steps. *Schedule the free steps first.*

4. Small steps are just like footsteps: Take one small step and take another small step after it. Keep taking small steps. *Because they're small, you can invent small steps to do every day and fit them around your routine.*

5. Small steps are just small steps. They don't rely on luck, on other people, or on results. *This kind of time management is supposed to be stress-free not stress-full. Break it down, schedule it, then (try to) let go of the results.*

6. Small steps don't necessarily go in a straight line. Actions don't have to lead directly to the next action, as long as they all relate back to the task. *Once you know what the small steps are, you can use small chunks of time or you can cluster tasks together.*

7. Take lots of small steps, especially at the beginning. *Add your small steps to your day-to-day, week-by-week, month-by-month routines; If necessary, analyse your peaks and troughs over the year so you know when to begin a project.*

8. Turn up. Small steps require you to get off the sofa, unless lying on the sofa is important to your goal. *Give yourself the time and the space to do what you want to do.*

9. Once you've prepared, you can do small steps – by adding them to your existing routine – without even thinking about the bigger picture. *Schedule some preparation time and some review time. The rest of the time, take the small steps – don't analyse.*

10. Small steps deserve to be appreciated. Pause at regular intervals to acknowledge your progress and to keep in check. *Use your journal to look in detail at how you use your time and to evaluate after the event.*

*A review of time-management methods*

I haven't included a whole chapter reviewing existing time management methods but have instead peppered those I've tried throughout the whole of this book or included them in the resources section. Here's a quick summary of those I've found most useful:

# 9: SMALL STEPS TO TIME MANAGEMENT

- David Allen's *Getting Things Done*. To follow David Allen's advice, start by piling up everything you need to do and go through it. Do anything that can be done in 2 minutes. Action everything else. There's much more detail in his book, of course. I recommend reading it if you are snowed under, or if managing information is as important as managing your time.
- The sections on 'How to Rule the Office' and 'How to Get More Done' in Oliver Burkeman's *Help!* offer practical and down-to-earth time-management tips. Here's an interview with Burkeman about his more recent book *Four Thousand Weeks*: https://www.theatlantic.com/family/archive/2021/08/oliver-burkeman-advice-time-productivity/619723/
- The Pomodoro Technique, created by Francesco Cirillo, will help you to know about the Pomodoro Technique as you work through this section. You can find out more about it via the Pomodoro website. In this well-known technique, one uses a kitchen timer to time 25-minute bursts of activity, with no interruptions, followed by a five-minute break. It's called the Pomodoro Technique because the kitchen timer used by Cirillo is shaped like a tomato (or pomodoro in Italian).
- *Organise Yourself.* Ronni Eisenberg's book contains straightforward, sensible and down-to-earth suggestions for organising your life.
- Mark Forster's books *Get Everything Done and Still Have Time to Play* and *Do It Tomorrow* contain lots of tips for becoming more efficient and demonstrate his systems for organising and prioritising your tasks.
- Here's Brian Tracy on time management: https://www.briantracy.com/blog/time-management/time-management-tips/

*What next?*
Now you know all about how small steps apply to time management and you've got some resources to check out, we're going to look at the difference between productivity and time management and return to Warren Buffett's 5/25 rule, to find out what it can teach us about prioritising.

# Chapter 10: Productivity and Time Management

### About this chapter
Productivity has become something of a buzz word recently and it's often used in place of the seemingly more prosaic 'time management'. They're taken to be synonymical, as if managing one's time is always in service of proficiency and efficiency. In fact, the two ideas overlap but mean something slightly different as I'll explain in this chapter.

### What does productivity mean anyway?
Productivity refers to two things at the same time: efficiency and the ability to get the results you want, with a focus on the results, or 'products', of your labour. As Oliver Burkeman points out in his recent book *Four Thousand Weeks*, if we're not careful we'll start to think that any labour that doesn't produce results isn't worth doing, or even that all our time should involve labour of some sort; that is, we should always be working towards a future reward. As Burkeman goes on to say, we fall into a trap of thinking that, if only we could get more efficient and produce better results, we could get everything done and finally be free!

The counter argument, he says, is that we're living our lives right now. We won't ever reach a point where the to-do list is finally finished and there's nothing left to do. If you're anything like me you'll find it fun learning productivity tips and tricks, but productivity has to be directed by our values and channelled into the areas of our lives where efficiency and results are important (I often use the pomodoro technique to help me get my marking finished, for instance, because it has to be done on time) and not those where it isn't (I have to remind myself not to try to 'schedule' too much on holiday or I won't properly relax). There's a

# 10: PRODUCTIVITY AND TIME MANAGEMENT

meditation on the 10% Happier App by Jeff Warren called 'Do Nothing' – which I love – but it's ironic I need an app on my phone to tell me to do that.

*Time management – or getting organised*
Time management, although it's become a euphemism for productivity, literally means managing your time of course. It doesn't refer to creating more time (impossible!) or reaching a state of perfect equilibrium (very likely also impossible for most people including me). In practice, it means organising yourself. In this sense, it's a catch all for executive functioning skills, like scheduling, timekeeping, punctuality, sequencing and prioritising. One of the reasons I went on a journey to find out more about time management and ended up researching it extensively – materials I shared with my undergraduate students at the time – was because I found executive functioning skills difficult, like many neurodivergent people. Let's face it: like many people do, especially when we're juggling busy lives.

Because of this, I view time management – or simply 'getting organised' – like a journey of discovery; it's not the end, the elixir that, if only I could find it, I would have everything I desired. Rather, it's something to learn about and experiment with, a process, a skillset you develop over a lifetime. As I've said before, it isn't possible to manage or control time. But you can organise what you do with your time, to a certain extent, so that you can fit in the things you love to do or really want to do. In sum:

- Productivity = efficiency and results-driven
- Time management = organising your time (actually organising yourself!)

Whether you think in terms of productivity or time management or both depends on which of these is important:

- Results and efficiency
- Getting organised

And the key trick – as Burkeman reminds us – is to avoid treating everything as if it needs efficiency, results and / or organisation!

*Do goals need productivity?*
How does all of this figure when it comes to goal setting? Don't goals always need an element of productivity? No. Goals aren't always results driven and don't necessarily have an identifiable end point. You don't necessarily need to get more efficient to achieve the goal and the goal may be a reward in itself, meaning there's an intrinsic motivation to keep it up. It depends on the goal.

*Two example goals*
For example, one of mine – 'spend more special time with my family' – is a goal that is a reward in itself and doesn't require extra efficiency. I could make a list of what I consider 'special' (beach walks, talking over dinner, going for ice cream) and tick off how much time I spend with them each week, but that doesn't feel necessary. That might be different for someone else. To me, 'spend more special time with my family' doesn't require productivity.

What about 'go swimming once a week', another of my goals? Does that need an element of productivity? It would if I wanted to swim the channel, or learn to scuba dive, or simply improve my technique. It helps to think about the goal behind the goal. Why do I want to 'go swimming once a week'? To relax, to have time away from a keyboard, to get fitter? Do any of those things come with an element of productivity? Actually, simply by turning up at the swimming pool and swimming every Saturday morning I am taking small steps towards all of those goals. Using *accountability* helps – my son goes swimming at the same time, providing impetus – but that's not the same as *efficiency*. Arguably turning up at the swimming pool is a 'result' but I'm not aiming for my results to get any better.

However, 'spend more special time with my family' and 'go swimming once a week' both require organisation – or time management. After reading about productivity and executive functioning over several years now, I'm certain that:

## 10: PRODUCTIVITY AND TIME MANAGEMENT

- Some areas of our lives don't need goals at all, and this changes over time.
- Goals don't always need productivity.
- Goals always need time management.

All of that brings to mind an obvious question. When you are goal setting, how do you identify which you need – results and efficiency or organisation and better executive functioning? Here are some ideas.

*The novel, the journal and the piano lessons*
I've talked about SMART goal setting before, and how, in many iterations of the acronym, the 'm' stands for 'measurable' and the 't' for 'time-bound'. For certain kinds of ambitions, it pays to use SMART or SMARTER goals. Let's say a fictitious goal-setter wants to write a novel and get it published. It would make sense for her to make her goal measurable and time-bound. Afterall, once she has set up the goal, she can forget about the ultimate outcome and simply take small steps towards it. She can decide how to measure her progress and when she wants to send a completed draft out into the world. When she checks in, separately, she can decide whether those targets are working.

Now let's say another goal-setter wants to start a journal about his life, a scrapbook of memories, photos, and short pieces of life writing, that he could one day pass on to his grandchildren. Yes, he needs to turn up and write it or otherwise compile the journal – and to do so regularly otherwise he won't do what he has set out to do – but the goal doesn't need to be 'measurable' and 'time-bound' in quite the same way. Those ideas don't quite fit the goal. He might want to have a looser target, in other words. *On Sunday afternoons I'll write in my journal*, for instance. He might keep the journal somewhere he can see it to remind him or 'habit stack' it with his afternoon cup of tea. The process is important, he wants to do it regularly, but the journal doesn't have a beginning, middle and end like a novel and he doesn't know when it'll be done. He doesn't need to be efficient.

When writing the novel, our writer might well keep a check on how many words she is writing in a session – if that's something that motivates her – or how many writing sessions she's managed in a week or a month. When writing in a journal – something more ponderous – that's probably not going to help.

Let's consider learning to play the piano in the second half of your life. It's something I've always wanted to do. Should I make it a SMART goal? It helps to come back to the idea of the goal behind the goal at this point. Why do I want to learn to play the piano? What's my motivation? If I'm going to find someone to teach me, I could turn that into a SMART goal. Likewise, if I want to make sure I practise a certain number of times a week. But could it be that in some situations, having a SMART goal would make me less likely to learn the piano? Perhaps because it appears to remove the need for intrinsic motivation.

Arguably, in all three cases – writing a novel to get published, keeping a journal to pass on to the grandchildren, learning the piano in the second half of life – time management is important. Productivity is only important when:

- what the desired result looks and feels like is externally designed,
- and / or having a beginning, middle and end is vital to the whole project's success,
- and because of all that, having a deadline is desirable, and may also be externally imposed.

## How to prioritise

We looked at Warren Buffett's 5/25 rule earlier, and now is a good time to revisit it. Remember the scenario: he tells Mike Flint, his pilot, to write down 25 goals, pick his top 5, and discard the rest until those 5 are done.

Warren Buffett's 5/25 rule is treated like productivity advice, but it's actually about prioritising what's important and making sure you do it. In fact, lots of advice about improving executive functioning skills is framed as if it's productivity advice but would be better titled with the slightly less slick 'how to get organised'.

Is learning to play the piano a priority for me right now? No. If I

## 10: PRODUCTIVITY AND TIME MANAGEMENT

were using Warren Buffett's 5/25 rule I would need to avoid the piano like the plague!

*Prioritise based on your life roles*
Michael Hyatt, in *Living Forward*, suggests using life roles both to set and prioritise goals. So another, non-Buffett, way to prioritise is *to prioritise life roles first*. For instance, arguably the most important role is looking after yourself – you could refer to it as the 'me caretaker' role – not for selfish reasons, but because without it you can't help anyone else or focus on any of your goals. You might also prioritise 'family member' or 'writer' or 'football coach' for example. The idea is that you set a goal for each and make sure they chime with your personal values. You only need prioritise the role for a limited period of time. Choose between 3 months to a year.

If you play lots of roles in life, at home, at work, in your wider family, in your community, in your friendship circles, due to interests and hobbies, then it may be hard to prioritise a role.

If this is the case, I suggest combining the life roles / values approach with the 5/25 rule in order to prioritise. Write a goal for each role, check they chime with your personal values, then pick the top 5 goals, no matter which roles they are associated with, and focus only on them until they are done.

### Productivity advice

Once you've worked out which goals need both time management *and* productivity – do that first – you can apply productivity advice; that is advice that genuinely helps you become more efficient and to get better results.

In *Peak,* Anders Ericsson and Robert Pool discuss how, in order to improve at something, we need to be able to identify our weaknesses, so that we can employ what Ericsson calls 'deliberate practice'. Deliberate practice means working on our weak spots and making them better, rather than simply doing our thing – when we will tend to do what we're already proficient at, because we're good at it, and being good at something is usually fun. Deliberate practice needs either a high level of self-awareness, a teacher, or a clued-up peer group, willing to give honest feedback, or preferably all three. In sum:

- One way to get more efficient at something, is to become more proficient at it.
- We become more proficient at a skill using deliberate practice.
- We therefore need a way to identify what we need to practise.

Another way to become more efficient at something is to focus in on the components of the task itself and your context when you're doing it, making both work in your favour.

- What's uncomfortable or difficult?
- What takes longer than it needs to?
- What gets in the way of me doing it?
- Are there any mundane tasks I could do differently?
- What could I delegate?
- What's the space like?
- How long does it take to get set up?
- Does my equipment need updating?
- Are there any small steps that I genuinely need to take first in order to make this process more efficient?

*Facing up to procrastination*
Last but not least, we become more efficient by facing our procrastination. Whole books have been written on the subject, but here's some of the best advice I know about:

1. Work out what you're getting out of procrastinating. What are you gaining? And what's the disadvantage? For instance, I work well to tight deadlines so often procrastinate until I can feel the pressure of the deadline. Unfortunately, this also leads to stress, aches and pains, and fatigue.
2. If you genuinely don't want to do the task, what is it that you don't like? How do you feel about it? Are you disgusted? Afraid?

## 10: PRODUCTIVITY AND TIME MANAGEMENT

Ashamed? Bored? Unappreciated? Tired? Overwhelmed? Once you know what you don't like you can address the problem, at least partially.
3. If you genuinely do want to do the task, what is it that you like? How do you feel about it? Are you afraid you won't get it 'right' or even that you won't do it 'perfectly'?

This level of awareness will help you to face (rather than ignore) the procrastination. The issue is rarely (if ever) that we're 'just being lazy.' If all else fails, try combining 10-minute bursts of the task with accountability. Get someone to check on you!

It depends on the goal, but in cases of perfectionism, going to a class or a group may help, as a kind of exposure task, because that provides an external deadline (turning up each week) and accountability (the tutor / group members), and you'll have to practise and make mistakes.

*Indistractable* by Nir Eyal, *Deep Work* by Cal Newport and *The One Thing* by Gary Keller have been useful when considering how I can become more efficient, avoid distraction and focus on what's important to me, and therefore get better results. In particular, *Deep Work* helped me to consider my values and the 'why' behind my goals.

*What kind of goal is it?*
Take two of your goals – perhaps ones that contrast with each other somehow – and answer the following questions for each.

- Is this a habit goal? I want to do yoga regularly, for example.
- Is it a goal with an end point? I want to pass my driving test, for example.
- Does the desired result look and feel like it is externally designed?
- Is having a beginning, middle and end vital to the whole project's success?
- Is a deadline desirable and / or externally imposed?
- Does it make sense to turn it into a SMART goal? (Remembering you can be flexible with how you measure your progress.)

GOAL SETTING AND TIME MANAGEMENT

*Here's how it might work:*
- Habit goal: I want to do yoga regularly. The wording of the goal is important, remember! This goal isn't 'I want to use hot yoga to lose 10 lbs' – if it were then it would be an end point goal rather than a habit goal.
- End point goal: I want to pass my driving test.
- Does the desired result look and feel like it is externally designed? Yoga: no desired result aside from turning up. Driving: passing my test is definitely an externally designed result.
- Is having a beginning, middle and end vital to the whole project's success? Yoga: no. Driving: yes – I need to start, improve, and be good enough by the test date.
- Is a deadline is desirable and / or externally imposed? Yoga: no. Driving: yes.
- Does it make sense to turn it into a SMART goal? Yoga: possibly to start with. Driving: yes.

*5 things this year*
Like Warren Buffett's 5/25 rule? You might like to revisit it now. The exercise is in chapter three. Once you've completed that – checking that the goals you've chosen are the right ones for you right now – do a 'this year' version:

- Write down all the things – related to your goals – that you want to get done this year.
- Circle or underline 5 of them.
- Write these in your diary or on your calendar.
- Destroy the list.
- Do everything you can to do these 5 things. When you've done them, repeat the exercise.

*5 things this week*
You might also like to try a 'this week' version of the exercise:

- Write down all the things – related to your goals – you want to get done this week.

## 10: PRODUCTIVITY AND TIME MANAGEMENT

- Circle or underline 5 of them.
- Write these in your diary or on your calendar.
- Put the list somewhere you won't see it. (You could keep it in a notebook, or the digital equivalent, used specially for capturing items for your Action List.)
- Return to the list only when those 5 things are done.

*Prioritise by role*
You already have a list of the roles you play in life, with related goals. If you'd like to do another review at this point, check these goals still chime with your values.

- Decide which of the roles to prioritise.
- Rephrase your goals if necessary.
- Decide on the timeframe.
- If you have lots of life roles and it's hard to prioritise, write a goal for each, then discard your list of roles.
- Apply the 5/25 rule.

Forget about any goal that isn't in your top 5. You'll still be in the role – you don't have to resign your job or stop coaching the football team – but you'll only be working on the 5 goals you've chosen.

*Work out what you're getting out of procrastinating.*
Over a week, identify several times you procrastinated. If you're a chronic procrastinator, you might well be able to come up with examples without doing this week-long research. If so, write them down. Now answer these questions. You may have to think quite deeply before the answer comes or ponder them for a bit then go for a walk or do something else to let your brain mull them over.

- What did I get out of procrastinating? What did I gain?
- Did I want to do the thing or was it unpleasant? Why was it unpleasant? How did I feel about it?
- How do I feel about doing a bad or mediocre job? Am I waiting for the 'perfect' conditions?

- What was I doing when I was procrastinating? Does this distraction task need scheduling for another time?
- Did or does accountability (someone checking up on me!) help me to stop procrastinating?

Once you've answered those questions, keep on asking 'why' until you get to the nub of the issue.

*What's next?*
We've discussed what productivity is and whether you need it (or not) and discovered that goals always need some time management – which simply means getting organised – and we've also taken a quick look at some of your reasons for procrastinating. Now it's time for another case study. This time we'll look at someone about to return to university and someone else who wants to find time to write a novel – and look at small steps time management in action.

# Chapter 11: Small Steps Time Management In Action

### About this chapter
In this chapter we meet two goal-setters, Mrs Brown and Mr Green, and two different kinds of goal. Then I go over some time management basics, the things you need to get to grips with in order to handle any kind of project or task where time management is important. We'll go onto some specifics, again using Mrs Brown and Mr Green as examples, and finish with some practical exercises, where you get to practise 'breaking it down' and working out a timeframe.

When you're applying the ideas in this chapter to your own goals, remember to break the task or project down into small steps until you get to something you could achieve today. If you find it's impossible to create small steps because you don't know enough about it yet, create a research task as you did in the first section and break *that* down into small steps. Remember that asking for advice is a kind of research.

### Time management examples
*When time management is important*
It isn't necessary to manage every aspect of our lives with minute-by-minute precision. That kind of approach sounds hard to me – and also anxiety-inducing.

There are some situations where organising yourself successfully (or getting organised) is important and these situations come up when we are hoping to achieve our goals *and* get on with our day-to-day lives. Look into Stephen M. Shapiro's "eight secrets of goal-free living" for more on this idea. Let's look at a couple of examples where time management might become important: studying and writing a novel.

## GOAL SETTING AND TIME MANAGEMENT

*Introducing Mrs Brown and Mr Green*
Let's imagine Mrs Brown has made it her goal to pursue a particular career and for the career she has in mind, she needs to study at university level. In a way, her degree course is a separate goal, though it will help if she treats it as an overlapping goal and keeps her career aims in mind as she pursues it. She has applied and is about to start.

Let's imagine a second person, we'll call him Mr Green, has decided to write a novel. He's always loved reading. He's done a couple of short courses in Creative Writing and feels ready to start.

### Time management basics
*Consider the time constraints*
On a course of study, you'll be given a particular amount of study to do within a certain timeframe. Inside that timeframe there will be constraints such as essay deadlines and exams, term dates and vacations. Mrs Brown needs to consider what time commitment is expected of her.

When it comes to writing his first novel, it's likely Mr Green has no particular time limit in mind. There's no pressure to finish. In other words, the process hasn't been structured for him. He needs to consider his own time constraints and decide how much time to commit each week.

*Consider resources and information*
For Mrs Brown, the reading materials and course information are especially important. It's likely she'll been given lots of information at different stages, which is a process she needs to manage by keeping records. For example, student handbooks, reading lists and assessment requirements may be given out in advance or at the start of term or posted online. Without time management, it's likely she'll run scared from one deadline to the next, not covering enough of the course materials along the way and therefore not doing as well as she could have done. In other words, poor time management could actually affect her degree classification and her overall experience.

There are different types of resources and information Mr Green needs to consider. Firstly, research he does into the themes he's writing about. Secondly, any information about the writing community, in his local area and further afield. He might also want to look into training and information on *how* to write a novel and on *how* to get published.

Both goal-setters need to be proactive about resources and information: Mrs Brown has to manage the information she's given about her course and be proactive about filling any gaps – whereas Mr Green's needs to go out and find it himself.

*Consider time and space*
Both our fictional goal-setters need to make sure they have an *appropriate* space to work in. Mr Green needs to put aside some regular time to work on his book and therefore needs a space to write in. It's pretty obvious that dreaming about his book will put his imagination to work but won't get words down on the page. Equally, Mrs Brown needs to be proactive about putting aside time to study and about learning some study skills.

*Consider the context*
Both Mrs Brown and Mr Green need to consider their context: the people and things around them that will affect their studies: their family, their job if they have one, their accommodation needs, relationship, social life, and anyone they are caring for.

Context has such an impact on how we manage our time that neither Mrs Brown nor Mr Green can afford to compartmentalise too much in the planning stages. Remember that in order to dedicate time to something you must stop doing something else or become more efficient or more organised or stop doing something else. Now this might be something unimportant, like time spent lying on the sofa doing nothing – although lying on the sofa could be important for coming up with ideas – but it's likely both goal-setters will have to make sacrifices and also that Mr Green will have a harder job explaining this to his family and friends, just because Mrs Brown's goal has an external structure to it.

*Ask yourself: does it come with an existing structure?*
With any task, think about whether it comes with some kind of existing

externally-imposed structure – like a course, programme, work project, or artistic production – in which case make sure you are still *proactive* in your approach: don't just wait for it to happen to you! Or do you need to create a self-imposed time management structure? What challenges does that present? If you know you work better with an external or self-imposed structure, consider changing the approach you're taking to play to your strengths. You might like external structure in some areas and not others. For example, signing up to an exercise class might work better than exercising at home to YouTube videos – or the reverse might be true. Although I finished my first novel during an MA in Creative Writing, I now prefer to impose my own structure when I'm writing, but I do belong to a writing group that gives me some accountability.

*Two different approaches with common themes*
We have two different kinds of goals here, and it looks like they require different approaches to time management. Mrs Brown's goal comes with an existing externally imposed structure: but to get the most out of her course she still needs to be proactive about achieving her goal. She can't just turn up at class without preparation. Mr Green's goal relies on a self-imposed time management structure: the danger for him is that without an external structure, with no-one to answer to in the initial stages, it will be easy to skip writing sessions. This is one reason why joining a writing group can help.

*Key considerations for everyone*
Even though these two goals at first appear to require different approaches, we see some common themes emerging. Whether a goal comes with its own structure or not, we can apply the following to any time-bound task or project. These are the time management basics, the foundation of any other tip or technique. We consistently need to consider:

- any time constraints
- resources and information
- time and space
- context

## Time management specifics

*Prepare*

Mrs Brown can get as much information in advance as possible: key dates and deadlines, assessment requirements, her tutor's office location and contact details and reading lists. Mr Green can also furnish himself with information by reading books and magazines on writing a novel and by joining a writing group. He can prepare himself for his novel-writing project practically too.

*Action – take some small steps*

Start taking small steps as soon as you can. Mrs Brown could read through her reading list in advance. When I wrote my first novel I took one afternoon off a week. This amounted to two hours work by the time I got home, but it got me started – and created a timetable for me.

*Create a Master Plan*

Once Mrs Brown has an idea of how her first year as a student will pan out, she can create a Master Plan. Mr Green can also plan his year from scratch this way. A Master Plan could be a Mind Map or a chart or table or a plan of the year on a large sheet of paper. You can find out more about how to create a small steps Master Plan on this page of my website: www.louisetondeur.co.uk/writing-a-master-plan-a-small-steps-guide/

Once you've done your Master Plan, you can transpose it to a year planner, calendar or diary. You'll need your Master Plan for one of the exercises in the next chapter.

*Kick out any time-consuming habits*

This is where Mrs Brown and Mr Green need to look at their current lives and ask: is there anything I'm doing that I could stop doing? This tends to be a habit that isn't very important. If they leave out this step, and still pursue their goals, they'll find themselves not doing something by default, and it could turn out to be something important like time with family.

## GOAL SETTING AND TIME MANAGEMENT

*Ask for advice*
Advice isn't the same as information, and it matters who gives it. Seek out an expert – not necessarily a professional expert. You could simply ask someone who has trodden this way before. Advice getting is especially important if you don't know what to expect. Ask someone in the know about planning your time.

*Schedule*
Both Mrs Brown and Mr Green could block out sessions in their diaries each week to do their work. Then they can concentrate on turning up to each session. A session is either a morning, afternoon or evening, with breaks built in.

Mrs Brown can use the structure that exists at her university – the course structure, the tutors, the environment, the library, any study skills sessions – to plan her time. She'll also need to add her own independent study sessions.

Mr Green needs to create his own schedule. When I'm writing it helps me to act as if I'm going to work and turn up in my writing shed for a particular time. Most writers consider time constraints to be a good thing. For example, Mr Green can schedule his own deadlines, such as *send three chapters to an agent in January* or *enter a short story competition in November.*

At the beginning of each week, they can both set themselves small tasks to complete. *I will read X article on Wednesday afternoon / I will edit chapter 3 on Wednesday afternoon,* for example.

*Peaks and troughs*
With all kinds of studying there will be peaks and troughs in terms of pressure and deadlines. Mrs Brown can use time she *won't* be seeing tutors or attending class to read or study. They will both need to plan around their other commitments over the year. A year planner or calendar will help you to consider family commitments, deadlines, work, childcare, social occasions and vacations. Michael Hyatt uses the term 'big rocks' to refer to big occasions or events during the year and suggests you mark them out in your planner.

## 11: SMALL STEPS TIME MANAGEMENT IN ACTION

*Avoid distractions*
This is a tough one when there are so many things competing for our attention. If you prepare well, and schedule well, you can go a long way to avoiding this problem before it happens. Take a note of the things that distract you and – if they are important – schedule some time for them.

- Make sure you've done the niggles exercise.
- Carry a notebook around with you to capture tasks as they come up.
- Use an app to help with focus, such as Brain.FM.

*Delays happen*
Plan for delays. Both of our fictional goal-setters can work to self-imposed – and in Mrs Brown's case *earlier* – deadlines to give themselves a balanced and structured workload plus proof-reading time plus disaster management time plus I-left-my-work-on-the-bus-and-the-computer-crashed time. Crucially, ask yourself how long it took you to complete a similar project before. How long did it take you to read a novel of a similar length? How long did it take you to write 1,000 words last time you did it? Put (earlier) deadlines in a diary then work backwards creating small steps – what will you achieve one week before or two weeks before the deadline?

*Evaluate the process*
This stage often gets left out. Divide the year into stages, say three-month blocks to fit the seasons. At the end of each stage take time to evaluate how well you've used your time. What time-wasting habits could you avoid? Is there anything you have forgotten to schedule? Did you meet your deadlines, self-imposed or otherwise? Why / why not?

*Pack a spade*
We can apply these specific techniques to virtually any situation where time management is important:

- Prepare. What specific small steps can you take to prepare for your project?

- Action. Take a small step today.
- Create a Master Plan.
- Kick out any time-consuming habits you don't need.
- Advice. Make a list of specific questions and ask someone who's been through it before you.
- Schedule. Block out sessions – a morning, afternoon or evening – in your diary. Set small specific tasks for each.
- Peaks and troughs. Identify the peaks and troughs in your year. Work with them. Note your 'big rocks.'
- Avoid distractions. Schedule some time for them if they are important.
- Delays. Plan for delays. Work out how long it took last time or how long it took to do something similar.
- Evaluate the process.

To remember these tips – and also to emphasize the need for garden time – think of the mnemonic PACK A SPADE.

## Practice exercises
*Break it down and work out a timeframe*

Work out the *smallest* step you would need to take for each of the following. Creating a flowchart, drawing pictures or writing instructions are all fine. Use whichever suits you. There is no need to get down to a microscopic level. A small step is *something you could achieve today* – in a couple of minutes, half an hour, or during a morning, afternoon or evening session. Remember the easiest way to work out specifically how long something will take is to think about something similar you've done before. Leave a blank space or add 'research' if there are any gaps in your knowledge. For number 5, pick one of your biggest dreams and break it down into small steps.

1. Small steps to apply for a job.
2. Small steps to launching a TV Channel.
3. Small steps to swim the channel.

## 11: SMALL STEPS TIME MANAGEMENT IN ACTION

4. Small steps to travel the world.
5. Pick Your Own Dream

Once you've worked through all five, go back and work out a timeframe. Based on what you've written, how long would each goal take? Don't evaluate. If it's 20 years, write 20 years. For the purpose of the exercise, it doesn't matter if you don't think you could do it, work out the steps. We're practising!

*What next?*
You've looked at a couple of case studies based on our two fictitious goal-setters, Mrs Brown and Mr Green, and you've had a go at some practical exercises that encourage you to think creatively about your time. Next we're going to discuss at how you would spend 1440, 10,080 and 525,600 – in minutes rather than pound sterling – and we'll take a deeper dive into how you go about fitting small steps into your routine.

# Chapter 12: I Wanted to Change the World But I Could Never Find the Time: Time Management and The Overworked

**About this chapter**
The following exercise regularly came up in school assemblies when I was small: someone has just handed you £1440. Plan how to spend it. The idea behind this exercise is that we have 1440 minutes in every day. Awareness helps us to spend at least some of them wisely. In this chapter I've applied the £1440 principle to a typical day, week and year, giving you practical exercises to do to look at how you could fit in some small steps towards your goals. I begin by talking about the rhythms and hotspots of life and finish by looking at signposting over a year.

**Rhythms and hotspots**
*The rhythms of life*
A day, a week, a year, a lifetime. Each of these has a rhythm to it. Each has a beginning, middle and end. Each most likely has moments of sadness and joy, mundaneness and wonder. Each has rest times and active times, times for your physical needs, time for family, time for work, time for leisure. Both a year and a lifetime have seasons to them.

*Think about a typical day*
Here's an example. This day has a definite a rhythm to it. Imagine it takes a fictitious person, let's call her Carol, a while to get going in the morning.

- Carol makes breakfast for the kids and packs them off to school.
- She still feels sleepy on the train to work.

## 12: TIME MANAGEMENT AND THE OVERWORKED

- Maybe she's at her desk with a coffee by 9 but doesn't really get into her work until 10.30.
- She has a meeting at 11 – she's on fire, comes up with lots of ideas and gets noticed by her colleagues.
- Carol has a lunch break at 1.30. Until lunch she's confident and breezes through her work easily.
- After lunch she has a sleepy couple of hours.
- Then it's wind down time before the commute home, when she's too tired to read the report she's promised to review before tomorrow.
- Carol spends some time with her family, cooks and eats dinner and watches a bit of TV.
- She starts to feel tired as she's sipping a glass of wine in front of a film and nods off at about midnight.

Stop and make some notes in your journal. How could Carol make things easier for herself?

*Rhythms and hotspots: a practical exercise*
Once you know what your rhythms are, time management is much easier to deal with. It's no longer a system that you impose on your life or your particular goal. Rather you can incorporate it, realistically, into your week. You're going to introduce some awareness into your week. For the next 7 days, record the rhythms of your days. We'll use this information later.

1. Record the following:
   - Base your record on the *kind* of activity you are doing – use the life categories we've talked about previously.
   - Add your energy levels: how active or restful you feel on a scale of one to ten, one being asleep and ten being vigorous activity or hard work.
   - Attempt to record your fluctuating emotions – note down how you *feel* about particular tasks. This is tricky because the act of writing it down often changes the emotion!

2. Added extras: stress points. There are certain times during the day when we might feel tense or angry, find it difficult to cope, or which we find particularly stressful. You might also feel particularly hungry or sleepy at certain points. Try to identify these hotspots as you create your rhythm diary.
3. Added extras 2: family hotspots. In common with many families apparently, our family has a particular hotspot at the end of the working day when we finish work and segue into cooking dinner. Getting out of the house at the beginning of the day is another common hotspot. What are your family hotspots, if relevant?

*Making the hotspots easier*
What small steps can you take to make your hotspots easier? Until we realised that we needed some transition time from the workday to the evening – and also to unwind – it was a source of tension. We planned how to cope with it with simple, small steps. We don't do them all religiously, of course: a change of clothes perhaps, a sit down, a glass of water, some time alone, some time catching up *before* starting to cook. One small thing that helped us get out of the house in the morning when our son was small was a basket. We put keys, bus passes, ID badges and anything that was likely to get lost in the basket. Then we could grab and go before we left.

## 1440 minutes
*1440 minutes: practical exercises*
1. What are you doing with yours? Every day you get 1440 minutes to spend. What did you do with yours yesterday? Be as specific as you can. (A difficult task – it's easy to forget how we use our time.)
2. A detailed day-in-the-life. Pick a day when you know you'll have a little bit of leeway to stand back and observe. Not the day of your wedding or driving test or house move or something equally stressful! Nothing too action-packed going on. Record everything

## 12: TIME MANAGEMENT AND THE OVERWORKED

you do, with the time it takes you. Carry a small notebook. You'll have to do this as you go along: it'll be impossible to remember afterwards in enough detail.

3. Specifics: I'm not implying that any of these things are wrong, far from it, but once you've completed the detailed day-in-the-life activity, look at how much time you spend on specific things. In particular, look at how much time you spend watching TV, preparing and eating meals, sleeping, chatting, staring into space, clearing up. Now look at how much time you spent on:
   - things that *weren't planned*
   - things that were unimportant or unnecessary
   - things that related to the goals you've set, directly or tangentially.

*Finding room inside 1440*

As I've said before, time management isn't magic. To find time for your goals you've got to become more efficient or more organised or stop doing something else or incorporate your thing into an existing habit. Organising yourself day-to-day means you'll need to take a step back to do some more observation. Here some ideas.

1. Get up earlier or go to bed later,
2. Delegate or share some of your tasks,
3. Leave work to work hours,
4. Pay someone to do it instead (to clean, to look after the kids, to do the laundry). This obviously creates a financial burden. Even if this is an option for you, it may require sacrifice. Are you prepare to skip your meals out so you can hire a cleaner, for instance?
5. Ask someone to do it for free (could Grandma babysit?) or arrange a skills swap – as long as this still buys you some time,
6. Move from full-time to part-time work or study,
7. Cut down your travel time (share school pick up duties, arrange to work from home, move closer to work)

GOAL SETTING AND TIME MANAGEMENT

8. Give something up. If you don't plan for it and just start doing something else, you'll automatically find yourself dropping something. When I wrote my first two novels, my house got messy and my social life suffered!
9. As a long-term strategy, take *longer* to do something. This happened by default with my novels. Because I couldn't work on them fulltime, each took several years to write, which I see as a positive thing – it gave them a chance to mature.
10. Get very good at efficiency techniques. Many time management strategies focus on becoming more efficient. Make it your mission over the next month to collect efficiency strategies – from the internet, from books and magazines, from your friends – and try them out in a playful way.

*Review your detailed day-in-the-life*
First ask *why* you want to find more time. Write it down. Then look again at your detailed day-in-the-life. *Aside from becoming more efficient,* where could you find a few minutes out of the 1440 you have every day to work on your goals or to organise your life? Take some time to prepare, then try it for a few days and record the results. Remember the chapter on reality checking in the previous section! Don't set yourself unrealistic targets. If you already get up at 6, it may not be feasible to get up an hour earlier.

## 10080: the number of minutes in a week
*Giving a week the once over*
We've looked at a day close up. Now we're going to give a week the once over. Remember these are guestimates.

- Assuming you sleep for 8 hours a night, you spend 3360 of your 10080 minutes asleep.
- Assuming you spend an hour over breakfast, lunch and dinner, you spend 1260 minutes eating. If you also spend an hour preparing and clearing up each meal, you spend 2520 minutes a week on food. By the way, this is a key area for delegation or sharing tasks

## 12: TIME MANAGEMENT AND THE OVERWORKED

or for time-saving gadgets. Could you pre-prepare food for the day all in one go? Would a steamer or a slow cooker help?

- Imagine that, between 8 and 11 each evening, you wind down, maybe watch some TV, play computer games or go out to the pub with friends: that's 1260 minutes TV or pub or gaming.

*My weekly count up*

OK, it would be excruciating to record the minute detail of your life for a week. You've already had a go at recording your week under 'rhythms and hotspots' so use that information for this exercise. Also, you can look at the detailed day-in-the-life you recorded and extrapolate.

1. The idea is to take a week and record in your journal roughly how long you spend on typical activities. Count your main activity of the day as work whether you're paid for it or not. Break this down into different kinds of work If you like. How long do you spend:
   - eating,
   - exercising,
   - looking after others,
   - relaxing,
   - shopping.
   - sleeping,
   - socialising,
   - traveling,
   - working?
2. Now add some more categories of your own. For example, in one week, how much time do you spend:
   - checking email,
   - in meetings,
   - on social media,
   - cleaning,
   - helping your kids with their homework?
3. Check your balance. This is a bit like totting up your bank balance. What did you spend most time on? Anything surprising come up?

*A week in detail*
Take one part of your life: one that you'd like to change related to one of the goals you've set. Keep a detailed record of it. For example, if you want to be able to sleep better, keep a record of your evening and night-time routine.

Another example: if you want to start eating healthily, keep a record of everything you eat and drink for a limited period. Try not to evaluate, just observe. Keeping a food diary helped me to identify the extra snacks that were stopping me from losing weight. Simply writing it down helped!

*Finding room inside 10080*
Sometimes we want to incorporate small steps every day. Sometimes once or twice a week works better. It depends on what our goal is. Have a look at your weekly expenditure of time.

- Aside from becoming more efficient, is there any time you didn't spend in the best way for you?
- Any time you could use for your goals?
- Again, be realistic. Don't cut out relaxation, for example. You need to wind down!

## 525,600 minutes and beyond
*A year in the life exercise*
There are 525,600 minutes or 8,760 hours in a year. Using the previous exercises take some time to work out (roughly) how much time you spent last year:

- working
- sleeping
- exercising
- going to supermarkets
- concentrating on stuff that's important to you?

*The rhythm of the year*
A day has a rhythm, as we've discovered, so does a week. All these

## 12: TIME MANAGEMENT AND THE OVERWORKED

things, along with the seasons – and the events and traditions associated with them – contribute to the rhythm of the year. The school holidays, Christmas, the long warm days of summer or chilly winter nights all affect how we feel, how we relate to each other and how we relate to the projects we are working on.

In your journal, jot down how these seasonal rhythms affect your goals. We'll come back to this in the next chapter.

*Your goals over a year: using signposts*
A year is a big enough chunk of time to enable you to work on a sizable project or task, but it is too big to hold in your head all at once. So we use signposts. A signpost is simply a point you want to reach by a particular stage in the year. Signposts are also very handy for reality-checking. When you create your signposts, think carefully about the peaks and troughs you've identified. If you haven't yet done your Master Plan – whatever method you want to use – do one now with the aim of transposing it onto a calendar or planner. A year planner makes it easier to conceptualise the progress of the project over the year, a calendar (with space to write on it) makes it easier to mingle your small steps with other tasks, appointments and commitments.

1. Take one goal and add signposts to your calendar or year planner in the following order:
   - six monthly signposts,
   - three monthly signposts,
   - monthly signposts

Alternatively, add a signpost every twelve to fifteen weeks, with a review every six to twelve weeks. If you find the process difficult, it may be easier to work backwards from the point at which you wish to successfully finish the project or achieve your goal, like you did in the one of the flowchart exercises at the beginning of this book.

2. Once you've put in your signposts, you can block out morning, afternoon or evening sessions so you can work on your project. Personally, I add these scheduled sessions to the family calendar

## GOAL SETTING AND TIME MANAGEMENT

*and* my diary, but you may not need to. At this stage you can check to see whether you've been overly ambitious or if you've under-committed. For instance, will you finish making the film you've always dreamed about by the end of the year if you only have one session a week to work on it?

3. Now decide which small steps you'll do on a weekly (or even a daily) basis. Put in up to six week's worth. Remember to add time to review your plan.

This technique also works for longer projects of, say, 3, 5, 10 and 20 years. For example: *In 5 years' time I will travel around the world* or *In 10 years' time I will have paid off my mortgage.* Put in yearly signposts, then six monthly, then three and one monthly signposts, or add a signpost every twelve to fifteen weeks. After that don't forget the crucial stage: block out sessions and create weekly small steps, with review time built in.

*Finding room inside 525,600*
Take into account the rhythm of your year and examine your calendar or year planner.

- Is there a point when you could take some time off to work on a particular project in one solid chunk?
- Is there a point when you could plan some special time with people who are important to you?
- Could you volunteer once a month?
- Go to the library once a fortnight?
- If you worked on your project every weekend for a year, what would you have to stop doing?
- Build in some time off, too.

*What's next?*
After doing all of those practical exercises examining how you use your time and thinking about how to fit small steps into your day, week or year, let's take a closer look at *when* you should be working on your goals. It turns out it's all about your body clock!

# Chapter 13: Circadian Rhythms

### About this chapter

Since writing the first edition of this book, I have joined the 5am club and left it again and have lived to tell the tale! What I discovered is that adjusting your sleep patterns and knowing when you have the most energy can help with goal setting and time management but not if you end up without enough sleep. So, what are circadian rhythms and how can an awareness of them help you to fit in time for your goals?

### What are circadian rhythms?

'Circadian rhythms' is the term used to describe the ebb and flow of our energy, our wakefulness and sleepiness, during the day. In fact, they affect most of our bodily functions, but we're most aware of them when it comes to our ability to sleep or wake up. They are impacted by light and darkness, exercise and when you eat. Circadian rhythms are controlled by an internal clock (actually nerve cells inside the hippocampus). If you've ever been jet-lagged, you know what it's like when your internal clock is out of sync with your immediate environment.

According to sleep researchers, you can be genetically predisposed to particular sleep patterns. Your 'sleep chronotype' is a set of inherited behaviours related to sleep patterns. The most well-known of these are the 'early bird' or 'lark' and the 'night owl'. You can take online quizzes to get to know your 'sleep chronotype' – but you may be well aware of it already!

You can also influence your body clock to a certain extent. For instance, by getting up or going to bed slightly earlier each night, or by exposing yourself to daylight or a lightbox. From my personal experience, I've discovered that sleep patterns change over time, too, and are heavily influenced by the environment, those I live with and work schedules, for example, and by when and what I eat, and how hydrated I am.

## Larks and owls

I was fascinated by Daniel H. Pink's 2019 book *When: The Scientific Secrets of Perfect Timing*. Early in the book, Pink describes the work of Prof Till Roenneberg, who he titles 'the world's best-known chronobiologist' and offers a simple way to work out your chronotype. According to Pink, you're either a lark, and owl or a 'third bird', that is, you're somewhere between the two. 'Extreme larks' and 'extreme owls' (very early risers / late sleepers) are rare. Before I relate what comes up next, then, a quick caveat: prior to any of this happening, I was – by Pink's reckoning – just about a third bird but with a high tendency towards lark! Although I didn't know it at the time, my 'sleep chronotype' was giving me an advantage.

## My 5am writing habit

When our son was a baby and a toddler (around the time the first edition of this book was published), like almost all parents, our sleep was disrupted. I regularly saw 5am not because of the sunrise or the alarm clock, but because I was already awake. During toddlerhood, he slept through the night, but he habitually woke up at 5. In order to get some sleep, I often went to bed at the same time as him. I found that as he began to sleep in later, my body-clock had reset itself: I was still waking up at 5 and he was sleeping till 6 or 7.

Being a writer, I decided to use this time to my advantage and get up and write, rather than lying awake staring at the ceiling. I should reiterate that it's still important to get the right amount of sleep. There are some members of the 5am club on social media who have a cavalier 'sleep is for losers' sort of attitude, which comes with a severe health warning! At the point I took up 5am writing, I decided that I would still try to get 8 hours, which meant sacrificing late evenings for early mornings. I was happy to trade one for the other because it meant I got my writing done.

The good thing about early mornings is the peace and quiet, when it feels like no one else is awake and nothing is expected of you. There

## 13: CIRCADIAN RHYTHMS

was no pressure for me to do anything else. Because I trained myself (at first by accident, then by design) to wake up at 5am, I didn't need an alarm clock.

*Habit-stacking and rituals*
I usually made a cup of tea first. I mentioned earlier that author James Clear talks about the importance of attaching new habits to existing ones – called 'habit stacking'. Michael Hyatt discusses making a ritual of the whole process. Early morning tea fulfilled both of these roles for me.

Sometimes I would get back into bed and edit a manuscript I had printed out the day before. In the summer I would head to my writing shed at the bottom of the garden, or work in the kitchen. I didn't add in any extras: I didn't go jogging or have a cold shower before I started. My goal was to find time to write, and the solution (for me) was to follow my chronotype and to use the peaceful time I had available at the start of the day. I usually managed to fit in a couple of hours writing before the day kicked in.

I have 'stacked' a few more habits on top of my early morning writing now I've been doing it for several years. It's when I prefer to do 10 minutes of yoga and 10 minutes of meditation too, because they help my mental health. As we're talking small steps here, don't get too ambitious with your habit stacking when you first try it. Take one simple thing (like an early morning cup of tea, for instance) and stack one simple habit on top of it.

Gradually, though, our son started to go to bed later. We live in a small house, meaning it was hard for me to turn the light out at 9. Over time, I started to wake up at 6 instead. Still early, but not quite as extreme. If my wife organised breakfast, I could still fit in two hours writing.

And inevitably, now he's almost a teenager, lights out has moved again, and anyway, for health reasons I find it harder to wake up earlier that 6.30 or 7.

*Is there anything special about early mornings?*
If you're an owl, you might be horrified at the thought of 7am, let alone

5. What's interesting for me to think about as a lark – and I invite you to do the same whatever your chronotype – is whether there's anything special about early mornings that late evenings couldn't also offer. I suspect that I'm biased in favour of early mornings and – just as I do in early mornings – owls would find comfort in turning up to do their thing late night.

You also need to consider collaboration. If your goal requires working with other people, early morning or late night alone time probably won't work. Alone time suited my goal (to find time to write when I had a young child) – does it suit yours?

Anecdotally, it's likely I inherited my tendency to be a lark from my mum (and from my maternal grandparents), whereas my dad was an owl. If you're still not sure of your chronotype, I recommend Daniel H. Pink's book, but you might also like to think about whether members of your family are early or late risers, when given the choice.

*Don't sacrifice your sleep*
Based on the reading I've done on the importance of sleep, I suggest that you focus on your sleep first before anything else. If you can only do one small thing to make your sleep better, do that first, then take another small step and another, before trying to adjust when you sleep. Put getting enough sleep before working on your goals – sacrificing your sleep may seem like the ideal solution to 'creating more time' but it will impact negatively on your life (and therefore your goals!) in the medium to long term.

## Working with your circadian rhythms
*The traffic light system*
Instead of trying to 'create more time' which is actually impossible, try applying the traffic light system, which I learnt from writing coach and author Sophie Hannah. A task is 'red' if you need maximum concentration and focus to do it. You'll probably need to be alert and on your own (or in the most optimal environment) when you do it. A task is 'green' if you can do it with other people around, despite interruptions, and

you can pick it up again easily from where you left off. This isn't the same as multi-tasking, by the way, it simply means the type of task that doesn't require maximum focus. An 'amber' task needs some degree of concentration – you'll want to keep interruptions to a minimum – but it doesn't need laser focus.

We're all different, so your red, amber and green tasks will be different to mine, as will your preference for being completely alone or having other people around or actively involved. But even though there's no definitive list matching task-type to colour, working out your own red, amber and green tasks will help you to gauge when in your day to do them. As a useful side effect, identifying 'green' tasks will allow you to take small steps towards your goals even if you are, say, waiting to see the dentist.

Based on the writing goal I've been talking about in this chapter, here are some examples of my own red, amber and green tasks:

- Red: writing a first draft of anything creative.
- Amber: editing a draft by hand with a pen.
- Green: reading a book / doing research.

Another goal of mine is to cook from scratch more often. Here are some more examples of colour-coded tasks:

- Amber: cooking a new recipe.
- Green: researching new recipes.
- Green: cooking a dish I've made many times before.

Combining the traffic light system with an awareness of your circadian rhythms means you could schedule red tasks for times of the day when you feel sharpest and green tasks for when your energy is more mellow.

## Cultural expectations for days of the week
*What's in a name?*
We've thought about your fluctuating energy levels during 24 hours, but what about over a week? In the last chapter we looked at what you actually do over a week. But is there a right day to work on your goal?

Is it better to grab a couple of evenings after work or spent time on your goal at the weekend? Or take a small step every day? It depends!

When I was at university studying Drama, I took an improvisation class (on a Friday – so ironically I will always associate Fridays with improvisation) and during the class we once had to come up with a way of identifying the days of the week without naming the day. The lecturer concluded that there was nothing essential about a day, no essence that makes Wednesday Wednesday-ish, other than what we've attributed to it. Ay, there's the rub! We HAVE attributed ideas / activities to certain days and the cultural and social pressure to conform to those ideas is still strong, even though it's liable to change over time.

*Sunday shopping and cultural newness*
In the 1980s, when I grew up, you couldn't go shopping on a Sunday. At my religious grandparents' house on a Sunday, you couldn't do very much at all! Many people still observe a holy day or Sabbath on one day a week of course. For me, Sunday still has vestiges of my childhood Sundays even now when I could buy practically anything I fancied on that day, and my grandparents have passed away. Wednesday will always feel like the 'hump day' of the week, even though I now often work at least one day at weekends. Saturday feels like the day to go shopping and do chores. These aren't stable or universal, but we all have a 'feel' for certain days of the week.

What's more, society likes to tell us what we 'should' be doing on certain days of the week. Start your week by planning for an hour on Monday morning, life coach Brooke Castillo advises. She calls this 'Monday hour one'. (I've linked to the podcast where she says this in the resources section.) Good advice – but it wouldn't work quite so well if we didn't think of Monday as a day of new beginnings! In her book *How to Change* behavioural psychologist Katy Milkman talks about using this cultural sense of 'newness' to your advantage: change is easier at the beginning of the month, year or week. In fact, she's run experiments to prove that it works – so Castillo is onto something.

*Sociocultural pressures*
Other examples of cultural expectations for days of the week include the idea that we 'should' kick back and relax at weekends or do something worthwhile, or we 'should' be winding down on a Friday. Bear in mind that you're not the only person affected by these pressures – they are cultural idioms and sometimes hard to push against. Think of someone (who isn't required to) going into work on Christmas Day – or insert the big cultural celebration of your choice – to get a sense of how strong these sociocultural pressures are.

Talking of Christmas, think again about the rhythms of a year. These might be cultural rather than bodily rhythms, but as in the Christmas Day example above, they have a powerful effect.

## Months of the year

In the last chapter, you looked briefly at the rhythm of your year, and you'll know from experience that a year has its own cultural peaks and troughs. In the UK August and the end of December are trough points. We can speculate about the reasons. It might be because:

- key people are on annual leave so no decisions are made.
- large numbers of people *are* kids, or have kids or grandkids, or work with kids! These are the times they're not at school. (In fact, parents reading this might be thinking that August and December are actually chock full of activities!)
- we're socialised to think in school holidays from an early age.
- festivals from the past – gathering the harvest and the mid-winter feast – still survive in our collective consciousness.
- we all need downtime, and it feels as though the long warm days of the end of summer and the shortest days in the winter are the natural time for it. We've evolved to eat, sleep and reproduce, not to do business 100% of the time!

*Using peaks and troughs*
You can either go with these cultural peaks and troughs or find the other

people who work harder in August and December (presumably to take advantage while the rest are on holiday) and connect with them.

When are your own peaks and troughs over the year? In other words, when does the pressure mount up at home and at work and when can you take a breather? When do you tend to have lots of work or lots of deadlines and when do things slow up? Does this help you to identify chunks of time when you could work on your goals? One way to think of time management, rather than taking small steps all year round, is to focus on periods during the year when you know things typically slow down – if that happens! Be careful not to put off your small steps indefinitely though.

## Circadian Rhythms Activities

Here are some exercises to do in your journal to help you use circadian rhythms – and the rhythms of a week and a year – to your advantage, followed by some resources, in case you want to find out more.

*Keep a log*
Keep a note of how alert or sleepy you feel over a twenty-four-hour period. I suggest doing this on a workday and on a day where you have more control over your time, if that's relevant:

- When are you full of energy?
- When do you feel most relaxed?
- Does your energy slump in the middle of the day?

*When are you more drawn to working on your goal?*
Fill in the blanks in these sentences to find out. Substitute a particular goal for 'on my goal' if you like. In my case, I would use 'on my crime novel'.

Early mornings are_____

The middle of the night is_____

When I think about working on my goal early in the morning I feel like / imagine _____

## 13: CIRCADIAN RHYTHMS

When I think about working on my goal in the middle of the day I feel like / imagine _____

When I think about working on my goal late at night I feel like / imagine _____

When I think about working alone on my goal, it makes me feel_____

When I think about working with others on my goal, it makes me feel_____

When I imagine working on my goal, I am in_____ [fill in the PLACE] and I am on my own / there are other people involved / there are other people around in the background [DELETE AS APPROPRIATE] and when I look at the clock the time is_____ [fill in the TIME].

*Try it out!*
If you have some flexibility built into your week, then put aside some time to experiment. Schedule your goal for 6am and work towards that wake-up time by going to bed 15 mins earlier for a week beforehand. Similarly, schedule time for your goal in the evening – still making sure you're getting the right amount of sleep. Try working on your goal after lunch for a few sessions.

Then grab your journal and review what happened. It may be that simply thinking about this exercise gave you a big clue to when you'd prefer to work on your goal! But if you're still not sure, trying all three (or your own version) then writing about the experience is likely to be revealing.

*Days of the week brainstorm*
Write down the first thing that comes into your head when you think about

- Monday
- Tuesday

- Wednesday
- Thursday
- Friday
- Saturday
- Sunday
- The weekend

*Peaks and troughs exercise*
In your journal, record the following. Where are your personal peaks and troughs over the year? When can you take a breath and when does work pile up? For me, work gets stressful when essay marking comes in. This is a 'peak' for me. I have to work very long hours to get it done. It is not a good idea for me to have another deadline at the same time. Knowing when your deadlines are allows you to clear everything else. The best way to do this is to look back on a time you've done something similar. If you've never had a year like the one coming up, you may have to estimate. Keeping a journal during a typical year will help you to review how you spend your time at the end of the year.

*What's next?*
You've learnt about circadian rhythm and discovered *when* you're most likely to get stuff done and be able to focus. Over the next couple of chapters, we're going to get to know the Small Steps Method at a more granular level. First of all, you're going to learn how to set it up, break it down and make it easy.

# Chapter 14: Set It Up, Break It Down, Make It Easy

## About this chapter
In this chapter we learn three crucial aspects of small steps time management: set it up, break it down, make it easy. The examples given in this chapter use pretty major goals like building a house, writing a novel and making £25000. But the *set it up, break it down, make it easy* strategy applies equally to everyday tasks and time management at work too, and to any of the goals you set in the first section of the book.

## Set it up
*Set up what?*
Some of your small steps will be about setting up your workspace and maintaining it and organising your life. Using the following guidelines, you'll set up:

- Your spaces
- Your lifestyle and your support network
- Your routine
- Your chores and admin
- Your equipment

*Your spaces*
For everything you want to achieve, and for all of your day-to-day tasks, make sure the space is set up as well as it can be. Think you don't need a space set up? Work with the main space where your goal, project or task will take place. For instance, if you aim to eat healthily 80% of the time for a year, your space is your *main cooking area* and anywhere you

store shopping and cooking paraphernalia. Space comes first because it's practical and it's fairly easy to take one small step.

*Think CHECK*
Your priorities for setting up your spaces are calmness, happiness, ergonomics, comfort, and – another mnemonic – KISS (keep it simple stupid).

- Calmness. Can you instil a sense of calm and safety in the space, rather than disorder and mayhem? Even if disorder and mayhem are important as part of your final project – you might be organising a carnival or a puppet show for two-year-olds! – there are at least some aspects, particularly in the planning stages, that will need some serenity.
- Happiness. I don't mean pleasure or contentedness. Obviously we can't feel pleasure all the time, although arguably having a lovely notebook or a photograph or another object on display that gives you pleasure will help you to feel connected to the space. Make sure there isn't anything about your space that, in the back of your mind, reminds you of something annoying or distressing. An empty notebook might make you feel frustrated that you haven't filled it, a photo might make you sad. As a general principle, keep your own and other people's happiness in mind when organising your space. If your office is the place you retreat to after an argument it won't feel happy. Sharing your new garage workshop so both you and your partner can work on projects equally is likely to make you both happier.
- Ergonomics. How user-friendly is the space you've set up and the equipment you've got? How easy is it to get at? Consider the small things: any tools you need, paper, envelopes, pens, notebooks, stamps and bigger systems such as filing. Is anything in the way? This applies to setting up the kitchen if you want to eat more healthily, too. Try to make it as easy as possible to make healthy food.
- Comfort. If you bang your head every time you go into your

space or your chair gives you a bad back or it's very cold, it will affect your relationship with your project. Eventually the project itself will start to annoy you because you'll associate it with a sore head, a bad back and feeling cold. As a general principle, it's *not* a good idea to suffer for your project. Psychologically speaking, the more uncomfortable it makes you, the less likely you are to continue with it.

- KISS. When it comes to organising our spaces, often experts will advise us to use particular spaces for one thing. For instance, keep the bedroom for sleeping. Sometimes it isn't possible or even preferable to do this. Instead, we can try to keep some spaces simple, even if others are cluttered. Or we can turn one room into two different spaces. I've heard of a novelist who writes in two genres, so she has two writing desks, one for crime, one for romance. All the same, keep your space as simple as possible.

*Your lifestyle*
We also need to set up our lifestyle to make time management easier. Take a look at your typical week from the exercise you did earlier. How structured or unstructured is it? How structured would you like it to be? You can use CHECK to set it up:

- Calmness. Make sure you build in some moments of calm – or at least moments of pause – into each day and each week.
- Happiness. Does your lifestyle make you happy? Sure, there will be challenges, but is it satisfying, does it allow you to stop and think from time to time, and do you have time for the people and projects that are important to you? What can you do about anything in your life that's far too stress-inducing or unsatisfying?
- Ergonomics. How user-friendly is your lifestyle? Look at your typical day and week again. Could you make any of your regular tasks easier to do? Could your journey to work, your social life, your exercise routine, cleaning tasks, or shopping habits get any more user-friendly? For example – and of course these won't work

GOAL SETTING AND TIME MANAGEMENT

for everyone – take the train to work so you can read as you go, shop online to avoid overspending, agree to a babysitting rota with friends, or go jogging so you can skip the gym fees.
- Comfort. I'm not talking about overindulgence in food, drink, drugs or consumer goods here. I'm talking about kindness. Are you being kind to yourself? It's well-known advice: do something nice for yourself every day. Is your life all get up and go or is there some cushion time? Yes, challenges make us stronger, but there's no virtue in suffering for no reason.
- KISS. Simplify your life and your living spaces as much as you can. Over your typical day or week, is anything more complex than it needs to be?

*Set up your support network*
It's easy to forget that we can be *proactive* when it comes support networks. It's also easy to feel pretty desperate about a lack of support network. A support network is about quiet chats or hanging out as well as having a good laugh or joining an organised group.

Stop now and answer this question in your journal: could you simplify your week to allow more time to simply hang out with friends?

*Set up your routine*
If it helps, make sure you have a record of everything you need to get done on a day-to-day basis and the *specifics* of any small steps that you would also like to achieve each day or week. You probably already have a list of these small steps elsewhere in your journal. If you've been working through the exercises in this book you should have a pretty good idea of what to include by now. Try the list exercise below if you need to work out how to fit your goals into your daily and weekly routines.

*The list exercise*
1. Create a list that includes the specifics of anything you want to do regularly each day. The idea is to create a *daily routine* which becomes habit forming.

2. Create a weekly routine. Use sessions – early morning, morning, lunchtime, late afternoon or evening – and write in anything you want to do regularly each week. Schedule anything that can't be moved, like meetings or classes or start / finish times. From experimenting with these routines, it should become clear whether you're trying to do too much. Adjust as necessary.
3. You might want to do two lists, one for work and one for home to enable you to treat work projects separately.

*Your chores and admin*
Set up your daily and weekly chores so that they become part of the routine and so that they are as user-friendly as possible. Everyone has admin to do, financial or otherwise. Build this into your weekly routine and it won't pile up.

*Your equipment*
For any goals you want to achieve, for daily and weekly routine tasks and for chores and administration, you need equipment, including stationery and storage space. Take some time to review what you need. Make sure you set it up in the most user-friendly way possible. Make it accessible and secure. This process doesn't have to be expensive. If you do need special equipment you don't have, try freecycle or eBay for example. Start off as simple as you can. In fact, see this as a simplification process rather than a complication process. What's the most simple and appropriate way to equip yourself?

Don't let lack of equipment stop you from starting out. The beginning of any project – the groundwork, initial training or research – can often be achieved for free or through volunteering your time. Keep a list of anything you need to buy as part of your research rather than i) splashing out immediately or ii) writing off the project as too expensive.

Remember that raising the money to achieve your goals can also be broken down into small steps.

## Break it down

*Breaking it down to manage your time*

Now you'll apply what you've already learnt about breaking down your projects, tasks and goals into small steps. You'll also read two examples of how this technique works in practice. Once you've broken down the task, however complicated, into small chunks, you should be able to work out how long it is likely to take and to plan accordingly.

Take any big task that doesn't fit easily into your routine and write it out in your journal if you haven't already done so. Naming it like this is a big start. Include notes on your timeframe for the task. What's the deadline? Or how long do you think it will take? How long did it take you last time you did something similar?

*The component parts*

What are the component parts of this task? Is anyone else involved? Be as concrete and specific as you can. For example, imagine a fictional person called Martin. His goal, simply stated, is *I want to build my own house*. It initially breaks down into research, design, finance, and possibly training. Once the project is underway, he might have new headings such as administration, project management, budget, infrastructure, plumbing and wiring etc etc. Naming the parts like this allows Martin to allocate time to each one and to work out how long each will take.

*Take steps backwards*

You need a year planner, desk calendar or a diary for this exercise.

1. Look at the big task you've identified again. Decide on the results you want. Where do you want to be? What do you want to achieve? Visualise it.
2. Start with the end result and work backwards. Each small step is something you could achieve on one day. Work out *when* you're likely to achieve what you want and *how long* you will need to spend on small steps each week. Have you got small enough? Have you gone far enough back?

## 14: SET IT UP, BREAK IT DOWN, MAKE IT EASY

3. If you find any blocks along the way or anything you need to research or ask advice about, make a list.
4. Take any apparent block. What do you know already? How could you get help? What would it mean to overcome this block? What would it look like? Again, take small steps backwards from the results you want. Write them down.

*Do you need any new knowledge or advice?*
Now Martin has broken down the task, he should be able to identify areas to research, people to consult, or knowledge and advice he doesn't have. For example, *I want to build my own house* leads to research tasks such as: talk to someone who's done it, find out how to buy a plot of land, find out about plumbing classes in his area.

*Something you can do today*
Remember that your aim is to break the task down until you get to something you can do today, noting any barriers along the way, including emotional barriers. For example, today Martin could spend one session finding online groups for environmentally friendly DIY homebuilders.

*Review your timeframe*
Now you've broken down the task into small chunks, review how long you think it will take. Look at the time you will need to dedicate to the task – over days, weeks, months or years – to do it justice. What's the monthly, weekly and daily commitment? Can you fit it into your routine?

## Break it down example: raising money.
*I need to raise £25,000*
This might well be the first, separate, goal when Martin breaks down *build my own house*. Imagine, for a moment, that time is no barrier at all. It frees you up to think creatively. You'll notice that its *time* that's the issue here, not your ability to raise the money.

Raising £25,000 is the same as raising £2500 10 times. Raising £2500 is the same as raising £250 10 times. Raising £250 is the same as raising

£25 10 times. (And of course, if you happen to be raising money for a good cause, asking everyone you know to ask everyone *they* know to give £2.50 – or to buy 5 raffle tickets for 50p – is a good start!)

*What could you do today?*
The prospect of saving up a large amount can be daunting, but you've got to start somewhere, and I bet you could do one of these:

- Find something in your house worth £25 that you don't use to auction online.
- Make a saving of £25 by cancelling a subscription or membership you don't use.
- Save £25 on your shopping by making a shopping list, downgrading brands, planning to use leftovers or making better use of your freezer, or find couponing groups on social media, or read a good book on saving money.
- Start a savings account and set up a standing order for £25 a month.
- See a financial advisor to make sure you're using money effectively and check out Money Saving Expert online.
- Save at least £25 by buying items you use a lot in bulk when they are on special offer. For instance, a pack of cards is cheaper than buying birthday cards year-round. Keep them in date order (by family member's birthday).
- Shop early for Christmas and other special occasions to avoid being taken in by attractive advertising. You can often pick up bargains after the event (Christmas, New Year, Halloween etc.) ready for next year.
- Save money at work by taking packed lunch.
- Do you have a skill you can sell, or could you learn one? Could make at least £25 from a skill you already have?
- Do an audit of your outgoings and find another way to save £25. (Look at what you actually spent last month, rather than what you're planning to spend next month!)

## 14: SET IT UP, BREAK IT DOWN, MAKE IT EASY

*Too much effort?*
It might seem like an uphill struggle to get to £25000 in £25 increments, but don't forget two things:

- You've decided that your goal is something you really want – if you've worked through this book then you'll have set a goal you're interested in.
- Reread the W. H. Murray quotation about commitment in chapter five. Once you commit, the magic starts to happen. Or rather, being proactive about money will make it work for you! 'Magic' might just mean using confirmation bias to your advantage.

*But is it worth it?*
Not everything we do can possibly have a numerical value attached – activities like spending time with our families, relaxation and doing the best we can to be healthy are all priceless. Having said all that, if your aim is to save some money towards your target of £25000, and you have a plan to earn extra – work out if it's worth it first. Here are some questions that may help:

- How much does it cost for you to live for a day, in terms of heating, rent, food, bills etc? Divide that by 24 to get the cost of an hour.
- How much do you cost in your day job?
- How much can you earn per hour, PAYE or freelance?
- How much tax would you pay on the extra you earn?
- How much could earn in the private sector doing what you do?

It may not be worth doing something extra that sees a considerably lower return for the hours put in. You've also got to consider how much *time* you will allocate to each new money-making project, including research and preparation time.

Delegation – because it saves time – can save money or free you up to earn more. Consider employing someone to do some tasks, such as cleaning, or to act as your bookkeeper or Virtual Assistant. How much are you 'paying yourself' to do the work? These tasks may take up time when you could be earning money through higher paid work.

There might be something more radical (and risky) you could do to raise money – of course with the advice and support of an expert – such as investing in property or stocks and shares or changing your job. These kinds of decisions can't be taken lightly. See a financial advisor first.

**Break it down example: writing a novel.**
*I want to write the first draft of a novel*
Imagine you plan to write a novel of around 100, 000 words. Once more, imagine for a moment that time is no barrier at all, because it allows you to think creatively. Assuming that you can string a sentence together, you'll soon discover that the issue here is not whether you are capable of writing 100,000 words, it's a matter of how much *time* you give to the project. You don't write that much in one go of course. You write however many words you usually write in one session, whether that's 250, 500, 1000 or 5000. You'll find that 100,000 words means:

- 100 sessions spent writing 1000 words.
- 200 sessions spent writing 500 words.
- 1000 sessions spent writing 100 words.
- Or think of it this way: if you write 250 words a day, you'll be close to your target by the end of the year.

*How to divide your time*
A novel needs at least four more things, and all of these need time too:

- Planning time
- Research time
- Editing time
- Marketing time

*Small steps to writing a novel*
I don't have space to go into these things in detail here, but note that *writing* time is separate from planning, research, editing and marketing time. Again, each is simply a matter of thinking up small steps, allocating *time* and turning up:

## 14: SET IT UP, BREAK IT DOWN, MAKE IT EASY

- Once you have given yourself the time and space to write, you can actually let go of the outcome and simply turn up.
- Of course, if you are working to a pre-existing deadline, you'll need to do the opposite. Divide up the time you have available and set up word length targets along the way.
- Make sure the time you give is appropriate. Remember that time management isn't a magic wand. To do it, you'll have to *not do* something else or become more efficient or more organised.
- To use this strategy, *you need to know how long it takes you to write 1000 words*, so I suggest taking a short course or doing some toe-dipping practice sessions before making the final commitment.
- Practice is much more important than talent. Practice is concrete and specific – you can schedule it, you can turn up. Talent is rather vague and hard to define. Also, it doesn't matter how talented you are, unless you practice no-one will ever know. For more on this see Matthew Syed's book *Bounce*, which I reviewed briefly in chapter seven.

## Using subheadings to break down tasks
*Mind the gap*
Many hands make light. Great minds think. Too many cooks spoil. Our brains don't like gaps and try very hard to fill them in – as yours probably just demonstrated with the last three unfinished sentences. You can put this capacity to fill gaps to your advantage using the subheading technique. By the way, it's easier to do after you've researched, read up on or talked to someone about whatever you're doing a little bit first, because you'll have slightly more contextual knowledge that way. Here's how you do it:

1. First divide the task into its component parts. If you don't know for sure, it's ok to guess at this point. Write them down in your journal.
2. Take a piece of paper and write out the task at the top. Use the space on the page to provide gaps for your brain to fill in.

Write the numbers 1 to 5 down the page. Under each one of these write the letters a, b, c.
3. Now think of five main subheadings relating to the task. Space them out down the page next to the numbers 1 to 5. Under each one – next to the letters a, b, c – write three mini-subheadings. There's something about leaving gaps (or telling your brain it needs to think up a certain number of things) that gets you filling them in.
4. Use your research or any expert advice you've received at this stage. If you know you'll have to write a business plan or seek financial advice, for example, then these can easily transpose into subheadings or mini subheadings.
5. Use colour coding to mark any gaps in your knowledge or any research points. Sometimes a task seems impossible simply because of these gaps. Create a list of research tasks instead. For example: "I can't do it. I know nothing about it" – very vague, and very negative – becomes:
   - On Monday morning, spend an hour looking into financial advisors in this area.
   - On Saturday afternoon, go to a Prince's Trust seminar on running your own business.

*Adapting the subheadings method*
- Use a giant piece of paper – as large as you can – and add images and colour.
- Create digital subheadings, in Word or on your phone, so you don't have to worry so much about setting up your page.
- Use more subheadings (1 to 10 for instance) and more mini-subheadings (a–e for instance).
- You can also successfully adapt these approaches and apply them to mind mapping. Have a look at Tony Buzan's work, which I mentioned briefly in chapter seven.

## 14: SET IT UP, BREAK IT DOWN, MAKE IT EASY

*Essay writing example*
The subheading technique works well for students who need to write an essay. Here's how:

1. First divide the essay question into component parts. Write them down. Go word-by-word through the question if you have to. For example, *How did the cholera epidemic in New York City in 1832 affect population growth?* Breaks down into 'cholera epidemic', 'New York City in 1832' and 'population growth'.
2. Check for hidden parts. Remember I said that it's easier to use the subheading technique after you've researched, read up on or talked to someone about whatever you're doing a little bit first? There are some hidden parts to this question – most importantly water and sanitation – that you'd only know about if you had a bit of knowledge about cholera outbreaks.
3. You need context. You're also going to need some contextual information about New York City and population growth before and after 1832. This is the case with most essays and is where your studying comes in!
4. Take a large piece of paper and write out the essay question at the top. Use the space on the page to provide gaps for your brain to fill in. Write the numbers one to five down the page, under each one of these write the letters a to c.
5. You can change the number of subheadings and mini subheadings to suit the essay length. Add more gaps if the essay is going to be a long one. Include fewer gaps if the essay is fairly short.
6. Now think of some main subheadings that relate back to the original essay question. Space them out down the page next to the numbers one to five. Phrase them as questions if possible. Under each subheading write some mini subheadings that relate to that section of the essay. These are going to divide into paragraphs. How many depends on the essay length.
7. Use course guidance at this stage. If the tutor has told you to include three things covered in seminars, or if you have to

include books by three different authors, then these can easily transpose into subheadings or mini subheadings.
8. Based on the word limit, how many words will you write on each mini subheading? For example, a 2,000-word essay could divide into 5 sections of 400 words, each with a subheading. Those 400-word sections could divide into 2 paragraphs of 200 words, each with a mini-subheading. You might decide to divide a 1,000-word essay into a beginning and end of 250 words and a middle of 500 words, or two paragraphs.
9. Check for connections and links between sections that you can make reference to. You could show those connections using arrows or different colours. How will you link each paragraph to the previous one?
10. Use colour to mark any gaps in your knowledge or any research points. Turn them into a list of tasks. For example: "This essay is impossible. I know nothing about it" becomes:
    - On Monday morning, go to the library and look up the rate of population growth New York City between 1800 and 1832.
    - Spend evenings next week reading the relevant parts of Massimo Bacci's book *A Concise History of World Population and The Cholera Years* by Charles E. Rosenberg.

*Any written piece of work*
You can use the same subheading technique to plan any written piece of work, including long projects. You can use it for websites, in house magazines, newsletters or brochures, for example. This book was planned and written using this subheading technique. I also use it for blog posts and for pitching and writing nonfiction feature articles.

By the way, if you like the subheadings method, you might like Randy Ingermanson who writes about building a novel using the Snowflake Method. First published online, there's now more about the Snowflake Method in *Writing Fiction For Dummies*.

*I want to build my own house*
In fact, you can use the subheading technique to plan any project at all

## 14: SET IT UP, BREAK IT DOWN, MAKE IT EASY

*because writing it down is a like thinking on the page.* Imagine our fictional self-builder, Martin, uses the subheading technique:

1. He creates numbered gaps on a sheet of paper and comes up with five subheadings.
2. Under each one he creates mini subheadings on specific aspects of the project.
3. Under each mini subheading he writes bullet points, or specific tasks with time-constraints, or describes an aspect of the project as it currently stands.
4. He marks up in colour any knowledge gaps or research points. This will help him to separate out anything that currently feels impossible from aspects of the project that he could achieve this year, this month, this week, or today.

*Knowledge gaps*
As with the essay, sometimes a project seems impossible simply because of knowledge gaps. Using the same principles, you can turn them into a list of tasks. So the vague and negative: "I'll never build my own house, I can't even change a plug" becomes:

- On Saturday afternoon, investigate beginners' DIY courses.
- Have a pizza night on Thursday and look into self-build mortgages.
- On the way home from picking the kids up from school on Wednesday, see if the library has any books on self-build houses.

## Make it easy
*All systems go*
In this chapter, we've talked already about how comfort and ease make it *more likely* that you'll get a task done. Using the CHECK system, you should have already set up your projects, tasks and goals to make them calm, happy, ergonomic, comfy and simple. Your projects will still be a challenge but this short final part to the chapter allows you to check that your systems really are as easy to use as possible. Here are some practical exercises and ideas to help you to make it easy.

## GOAL SETTING AND TIME MANAGEMENT

1. *What do you see? What do you use?*
   Sit or stand in your workspace. What can you see? Anything annoying, stress-inducing, upsetting? Get rid of it. Anything you never use? Get rid of it. Anything that needs filing? Sort it out. Could you make it simpler? Calmer? Happier? What do you use in this space? Is it easy to reach? Easy to use? Does it annoy you? Why? Is everything easy to use and easy to find?

2. *What bugs you?*
   Keep a bugs diary. We've did a shorter version of this exercise earlier in chapter eight when we looked at motivation and you wrote a list of small niggles that annoy you, interrupt you, frustrate you or prevent you from doing what you want to do. Do it again but this time carry a small notebook with you all day and note *anything at all* that bugs you, including trains of thought, if you can manage to catch hold of them, news items, bad customer service or the way you relate to people and they to you. Bugs can be more general, abstract and random than the niggles you wrote about before. You can't eradicate them, but awareness helps.

3. *What's difficult?*
   Focus on one day and record anything you find particularly difficult or complicated.

4. *Decluttering*
   Make it easy by getting rid of the junk. Spend some time recycling, swapping, and using online buying and selling sites.

5. *Use small tools*
   Stick up whiteboards and pin boards, put pens where they are easy to get to, keep ongoing shopping lists on the wall, put clocks and calendars where you can see them, make sure your keys are easy to find.

## 14: SET IT UP, BREAK IT DOWN, MAKE IT EASY

## Case study: Set it up, break it down, make it easy

*I want to build my own house.* Here our fictional self-builder, Martin and his partner – let's imagine this is Carol again – set up their spare room, break down the task and make it easy:

1. Setting it up. Martin and Carol are going to spend Saturday afternoons working on the project. Initially they need some office space. They set it up so they can get to their files easily. Martin picks up some magazine holders on freecycle and uses a box for library books, so he doesn't forget to return them. They create a collage of all the things they'd like in their dream house: it's going to be environmentally friendly, with a room for everyone in the family, a utility room and a playroom. There will be a treehouse in the garden. They keep this on their desk along with a picture drawn by their children. They stick up a whiteboard, so their action list is visible all the time.
2. Breaking it down. We already know that their goal initially breaks down into research, design, finance, and training. They break it down further and Martin decides to spend this year doing a plumbing and electrical course at the local college in the evenings. Carol does some weekend workshops on interior design. In the meantime, they try to get their finances in order by keeping on top of them once a week, seeing a financial advisor, paying down their debts and setting up a savings account. Carol usually makes small Christmas presents for family. This year they make extra and sell them. Martin confines his research to borrowing books from the library on the subject. Notice the couple's extra financial commitment so far comes down to paying for the classes and materials for the presents. Eventually – using small steps – the present-making turns into a small business.
3. Make it easy. Here are some of the things they do to make the process as easy as possible. Again, notice how there is minimal financial commitment here – these are all small steps:
   - Martin calls in at the library on the way back from picking the kids up from school.

## GOAL SETTING AND TIME MANAGEMENT

- They pick evening classes as close as possible to where they live.
- They sell old clothes on eBay, making it part of their routine to check in every morning. They declutter the rest of the house in a similar way.
- They set up a standing order to their savings account.
- They clear all the clutter within five feet of the desk, pile it up and sort through it over a weekend. Much of it goes to the recycling centre or on a recycling website.

*What's next?*
We've seen how Martin and Carol set it up, broke it down, and made it easy to get their housebuilding project started, and I've been encouraging you to think of your own small steps in a similar way. The next three parts of small steps time management are just as important – so are THESE and THEM, as you're about to find out.

# Chapter 15: Make It Count, Keep It Balanced, Think Whole Picture

### About this chapter
We cover three more crucial parts of small steps time management in this chapter: make it count, keep it balanced, and think whole picture. Under 'make it count' you'll learn four ways to make sure you're spending your time in the best possible way: doing whatever you're doing and being present, concentrating on the important stuff, staying task-focused, and flexibility. In the second section, 'keep it balanced', you'll be introduced to balanced time management and the importance of incorporating THESE and THEM into your schedule. (We'll do more on balanced time management in the next chapter.) Finally, you'll look at convergent and divergent thinking – first touched on in chapter two – and try some divergent thinking exercises.

### Make it count
*Doing whatever you're doing*
Making it count means focusing on the present moment. Buddhist philosophers talk about being present in each moment, exhibiting mindfulness, rather than drifting through life unaware of our surroundings or the reasons we're doing what we're doing. This means, rather than longing to achieve your goals so much that the present – perhaps rather mundane – task becomes an annoyance, do whatever you're doing fully, wholeheartedly. Being aware makes us *make the tasks count* whether we see them as ordinary or extraordinary.

Some of the following small steps will be familiar but they are easy to forget. Write them up somewhere you can see them if you need to. Each of the following small steps will keep you more aware of how you spend your time:

## GOAL SETTING AND TIME MANAGEMENT

- Take a deep breath before each new task.
- Take regular breaks.
- Set an alarm on your phone to remind you to drink a glass of water regularly.
- Fully experience at least one ordinary task a day, without doing anything else. Making the tea for instance.
- Giving yourself limited time to do a task – and focusing on it fully – tends to make you super-aware.
- Write down ten things you are grateful for.

*How do you define 'important'?*
Making it count also means doing the important stuff. Several self-help gurus suggest that tasks can be categorised as important or non-important, urgent or non-urgent. We tend to do urgent non-important things first whereas, so the advice goes, it's better to prioritize *non-urgent important tasks* instead. Easier said than done in an age of information overload!

One serious problem with this advice is how 'important' is defined. I've used the word 'important' over a hundred times in this book and have left you to decide what it means! Part of achieving balanced time management means working out what important means for you and doing it. But so that we can take this particular piece of advice seriously, it's worth looking at some slightly different meanings of the term:

1. The self-help gurus who urge us to do the important stuff first seem to mean that important = *chimes with your values*. In order to implement this advice, you need to know what your values are.
2. Important could also mean *the thing that most needs your attention right now*.
3. Important might also mean *a task that will make the most difference to your life and help you achieve your goals*.
4. Important is likely to mean different things at work and at home. If you need to work to survive, to a certain extent *whatever is important at work* has to be given priority while you're doing it.

## 15: MAKE IT COUNT, KEEP IT BALANCED

It follows that if you spend most of your time doing things that don't chime with your values you'll be unhappy, and that if you do a job – paid or unpaid – involving your personal values and the goals you've set, you'll be more satisfied with it.

We need to allocate appropriate amounts of time to each important thing in our lives. Preparation is key to this idea. That said, adopting *do the important stuff first* as a mantra does force you to become more aware of how you use your time.

*Non-urgent but important*
For this next practical exercise, assume that important = *will make the most difference to my life and help me achieve my goals*.

- Start by identifying at least four non-urgent but important tasks. Break them down into small steps.
- Allocate time to carry out each small step.
- Go through your diary and add them in advance.
- After a month, review what you've done so far and set yourself some more non-urgent but important tasks. Break them down as before.
- Eventually aim to do at least one non-urgent but important small step per day, preferably at the start of the day.
- Use your routine to limit the time you spend on urgent non-important tasks. Email and social media, for example, can easily get you embroiled in things that seem urgent but are not important.

*What about non-important non-urgent stuff?*
Have a cardboard folder and an app like Evernote for interesting articles, organised by topic if necessary, and for any materials (including your own ideas) that you'd like to keep but don't know what to do with. Also use them for any projects you'd like to complete that – at the moment – are non-important non-urgent. That way you (and your desk) won't get bogged down with non-important non-urgent stuff, but you'll be able to find whatever it is if it suddenly makes you curious. As well as the app, create a folder on your computer to store ideas and articles you've found online.

For example, I like to collect recipes. You could argue that my collection is important just because I like doing it. Fair enough. On the other hand, you could argue that this task isn't important. I wouldn't save my recipe collection if my house was on fire. I'm not a chef and I'm not planning to become one. It's certainly not urgent. Rather than abandoning my recipe collection or agonising over how important it is and descending into nihilistic-angst, I've just made it easy to tear out and store the recipes, so it takes a matter of seconds. I also have a recipe folder on my computer.

*What you're doing IS important*
Making it count also means the opposite. Look at it this way: what you're doing IS important. Sometimes we can mentally downgrade very important tasks and feel that if we're not directly earning money or we're not out achieving a whole range of goals, then we must be failing. This is especially true if we tend to apply a business model to everything we do. Depending on your situation, looking after your baby is important, picking up your kids from school is important, spending time with your parents or grandkids is important. Sometimes (again depending on your situation) it's better to concentrate on doing what we're doing, without trying to multi-task. This isn't a contradiction of all I've said about goal setting: instead, it's about time. There's time to do what you're doing now.

*Stay task-focused*
Making it count is about staying task focused. You've planned to use your time in a particular way – now do it. As much as possible, forget about personalities, blame, guilt and not feeling like it. (If you can't, jot it all down in your journal before you start.) Now, if you've set yourself a task and allocated a session to complete it, *keep coming back to the task.* Every time you wander off (either literally or metaphorically) come back, until your session is over:

- What is it, specifically, that you've set aside time to do? Each time you start doing something else – checking your email, logging

## 15: MAKE IT COUNT, KEEP IT BALANCED

on to social networking sites, washing up – come back to the specifics of it.
- Use the space you've set up to structure your task. Sit at your desk or get down on the yoga mat or hang out in your workshop for the full session. Give yourself a bit of time to bookend your session, to warm up or warm down, again using the space.

*Flexibility*

Making it count is also about flexibility. Sometimes flexibility is seen as one of those soft skills that everyone says they're good at but are ultimately very hard to define. We're probably all set in our ways to a certain extent, and in certain situations, and flexible in others. Here are some ways to develop your flexibility:

- Offer to cover for your partner, a friend or colleague and ask them to return the favour.
- Snatch little bits of time to work on a task (or to think about it) when you're waiting for something or queuing.
- Carry a small notebook, or the digital equivalent, everywhere.
- Carry a book about your goal topic.
- Do something different once a week: go a different route, use a new café, walk instead of riding the bus, wear your hair up, sleep on the other side of the bed, eat waffles for breakfast instead of fruit, use a different brand, buy tea instead of coffee.
- Schedule sessions in your diary and turn up for them but incorporate flexibility by changing the time of day if you like. Remember to review your plan every six to twelve weeks.

Some things are worth being stubborn about! Remember that you're trying to make changes to your daily, weekly and sometimes monthly routines, to incorporate your goals, so stick at it. If you always end up doing something else instead of the activity you planned, schedule sessions differently rather than berating yourself.

## Keep it balanced
*Your year pie chart*
First of all, let's look at how you spent your year. Think about the last 12 months when you do this exercise:

1. Either use the headings career, community, health, hobbies, family, finances, friends, learning, love, spirituality, travel, leisure, social life as life categories or the roles you came up with in the first part of the book. How much time do you think you spent on each of these over the last twelve months? Work it out by averaging what you do over a typical week and calculating an actual percentage of your time; otherwise, you have my permission to guess! Give each life part a chunk of the pie. Small chunk = not much time. Large chunk = lots of time.
2. Look over your year pie chart. Which life part (aside from sleeping) got the biggest slice of the pie? Are you spending time on each area that is important to you?

*What is balanced time management?*
There's no way that we can achieve all our goals at once or involve ourselves in every hobby and interest from animation to flower arranging to orienteering to sports coaching to zoology. Therefore, we need balanced time management. Balance *doesn't* mean trying to cram activities from lots of different categories, like pub quiz questions: art, sport, nature, science etc. To make the ideas behind balanced time management easy to remember, think THESE and THEM! All will be revealed below.

*THESE*
As we've discussed before, many time management strategies focus on enabling us to use time more efficiently, so that we can perform individual tasks more quickly or competently. Ok, but our health and general wellbeing is so important that it would be ridiculous to leave it of the mix. I've broken down health and wellbeing into **T**aking care of yourself, **H**ealthy Eating, **S**leeping well and **E**xercise. Remember the acronym THESE:

- Taking care of yourself includes relaxation, getting checked out by the doctor if you need to, doing something about stress, being kind to yourself. It also includes taking care of your social and spiritual wellbeing and looking after your relationships.
- Healthy eating will mean different things to different people but roughly translates to following the 80 / 20 rule, that is, try to be healthy 80% of the time; getting the rainbow of fruit and veg you need; knowing a bit about food, what you need and what it does to your body.
- Sleeping well, as a concept, is pretty self-explanatory though it's sometimes hard to achieve. Do some research so you know how to get a good night's sleep; create a bedtime routine and a relaxing sleep environment; don't repeatedly put work before sleep.
- Exercise. Be active. Walk, garden or swim or use YouTube, for instance. It doesn't have to be complicated or expensive.

*Healthy eating*

Let's take food as an example and apply the Small Steps Method. When it comes to food and health everyone is different and you should, of course, see a health professional if you need advice. We learnt in the opening chapter of this book that food is on the bottom rung of Maslow's *Hierarchy of Needs* meaning that we have to sort it out *first* before trying to achieve anything else.

1. What small steps could you take so that you could eat a healthy breakfast 80% of the time? For example:
   a. Make it the night before or in advance.
   b. Buy or make some healthy grab-and-go snacks every week.
   c. Put a menu on the wall.
   d. Get up a bit earlier so you can take your time.
   e. Keep a food diary for a week.
2. What small steps would you need to take so that you keep your blood sugar level balanced? For example:
   a. Do some research into G.I. foods or foods and moods at your local library or on the internet.

## GOAL SETTING AND TIME MANAGEMENT

  b. Carry some healthy snacks with you and take time to eat them.
  c. Where you can, switch from white to brown foods.
  d. Improve how you eat at work, especially the snacks you have in meetings and on coffee breaks when your mind is on something else.
  e. Add to your food diary. Identify the times you're most likely to get hungry and reach for a sugary snack, if you haven't done so already.

3. What small steps would you need to take so that you eat enough fruit and veg each week? For example:
  a. Change your attitude. Decide what fruit and veg you like so it doesn't feel like a punishment!
  b. Keep a fruit bowl in the middle of the table and on your desk at work.
  c. Use a liquidiser to add fruit and veg to sauces and to make your own smoothies. Try different smoothie recipes. (You can buy frozen smoothie mixes. I've recently discovered that the discount supermarkets often stock these at a cheaper price.)
  d. Look into fruit and veg deliveries.
  e. Add to your food diary. Tally up your fruit and veg count at the end of each day.

*THESE and other people*
You may also be involved in helping others to keep THESE in mind, especially if you're a manager, or you have a partner or a best friend or a family to look after. For example:

- Taking care of yourself. *"I'll stay at work until 8pm tonight to finish a project and I'll come home early on Friday and give my partner a night off, then I'll take Saturday morning for myself."*
- Sleeping well. *"No, I won't buy a new flat screen TV because we really need a more comfortable mattress."*

## 15: MAKE IT COUNT, KEEP IT BALANCED

*Making time for THESE*

When you're thinking about time management, when you're breaking down tasks, creating routines and allocating sessions, make time every week for THESE and you're likely to feel better about the rest of your tasks and will probably achieve them more quickly.

*THEM*

No, I'm not talking creatures from outer space. Pairing THEM with THESE is a quick way to remember that spending time with our friends and family is a huge part of keeping our lives balanced. Yes, 'us' would be a more accurate way to describe this idea but THEM and THESE gives you a handy mnemonic! When you're creating weekly and monthly routines, allow time to do things with the people who are important to you. In return, when you give people time like this, they (usually!) respect the sessions you've scheduled to work on your goals. Obviously allowing time for others encourages collaboration and communication too. Balanced time management means keeping THESE and THEM in mind when thinking about how you spend your time. Take some small steps today, for instance:

- Take time to *plan* to be with people rather than sitting back and letting it happen. Be proactive about it.
- Do simple and low-cost things like walks in the park or coffee and chat.
- Use a calendar to schedule meetings and activities and keep it in view.
- Use social networking or email to stay in touch regularly.
- Arrange to do a regular activity together. Take the kids swimming once a week, for instance.
- Aaron Craze, chef and TV presenter, appeared on Blue Peter to talk about his family's tombola. All three members of his family write down four things they want to do – giving them one for each month of the year. They pick one from a hat once a month and go and do it!

GOAL SETTING AND TIME MANAGEMENT

*All about THEM*

Here's a rough guide to planning your time with family and friends:

- Family. You can define family in whatever way you like but get some family time into your schedule once a day and once a week. As a rule of thumb if you regularly have no time for those closest to you, you're overworked and need to rebalance.
- Friends. As for your wider circle of friends, if you're pushed for time, plan one larger get together every six to twelve weeks – a cinema trip, a festive meal, a party, a trip to the pub. Twelve-week blocks have the advantage of being seasonal. If you don't manage anything else, organise a summer picnic, a Halloween party, a Christmas lunch, and a walk in the woods in the Spring, or insert the celebration of your choice – and at least you've managed to catch up with everyone!
- You and your partner. A great tip someone gave me before we started a family: give each other evenings off and spend one night a week together, even if it's just cuddled up in front of the television.

## Think big picture

*A bird's eye view*

This phrase is a metaphor for a way of thinking about life. Imagine you could hover above the world and see the connections between things: in your own life, the lives of those around you, in your community and in the whole world. Previously we've talked about contexts: the environment and the people around us affecting our behaviour and the baggage we carry with us through life. These are the things around us that will motivate us to act in a particular way. Now we're going to look briefly at a different application of the idea: being a divergent thinker.

*Convergent and divergent thinkers*

In the 1960s, psychologist J.P. Guilford discussed *convergent* thinkers who were able to think accurately and precisely and *divergent* thinkers who could connect a range of different disciplines and come up with

## 15: MAKE IT COUNT, KEEP IT BALANCED

multiple creative ideas. It's since been suggested that we tend to do one or the other, that we could be labelled a convergent thinker or a divergent thinker. It's probably more accurate to say that we use both kinds of thinking in different situations but are better at one kind.

A slight adaptation of these ideas describes big picture thinkers who are creative and can make connections between things easily and pits them against details people who are systematic and good at accuracy. Again, it's likely that we do both in different situations but are better at one.

A big picture thinker will have a tendency to over-connect and be surprised by how easily other people seem to compartmentalise. A details person might get so bogged down in detail that they can't see the whole and may be surprised by how easily others forget to dot 'i's and cross 't's.

When people who are at either ends of the convergent / divergent continuum meet they are might find it hard to communicate and may be mystified as to why they can't understand one another. Yet in fact they *need* the other's way of thinking to complement their own. A business will benefit from knowing about and using both ways of thinking equally.

*Divergent thinking exercises*
When we're looking for a balanced way to manage our time, there's a point at which we need to be systematic and specific about our goals and how to achieve them but also we need to take time to step back and do some big picture thinking. We tried to be as systematic and specific as we could about breaking down our goals into small steps in the first section, and also to look at the impact on our lives as a whole.

1. Now take a moment to apply big picture thinking to *the way you use your time*. Imagine you could hover over your life. Imagine you could take the roof off your house or look through the walls and doors. Go out a bit further and imagine you could do the same with your neighbours' houses. Now try your whole street. What about the whole town?
   a. How do you use your time?
   b. Why do you use your time in this way?

## GOAL SETTING AND TIME MANAGEMENT

    c. Can you spot any extra time you didn't know you had? (How long do you spend waiting in an average week, for instance?)

2. Are you really time-poor? Let's examine your time priorities. Keep in mind the exercises you did during previous chapters in this section and the definitions of 'important' we looked at earlier. Create two lists as follows:
    a. What's the most important thing you need to do today, this week, this month, this year?
    b. What else do you need to get done today, this week, this month, this year?
    c. How balanced are your two lists?

*What's next?*
In this chapter, you learnt how to make it count, keep it balanced, and think whole picture. You've also discovered how important it is to look after yourself and to use your support network. The acronyms THESE and THEM are designed to help you to remember to do that, and are just as important as SMART, if not more so. You've also had an introduction to the concept of balanced planning. We'll look at that in more detail in the next chapter.

# Chapter 16: Balanced Planning

**About this chapter**
In this chapter we look at two ways of planning your time: the hour-by-hour approach and a form of timetabling, using morning, afternoon and evening sessions. The chapter finishes with some tips on implementing balanced time management and some exercises to try.

**The hour-by-hour approach**
There are lots of ways to plan your time. One isn't necessarily better than any other as long as you make it work. Some writers of time management books suggest very specific scheduling. For example, *I Know How She Does It: How Successful Women Make the Most of Their Time* by Laura Vanderkam includes several examples of tightly scheduled days.

A more flexible (roughly) hour-by-hour plan, using different sized chunks of time, might look a bit like this:

7 – 8 get ready for work
8 – 9 drive to work
9 – 9.15 review diary
9.15 – 9.30 answer or flag any urgent emails
9.30 – 10 staff meeting
10 – 10.15 update PA
10.15 – 11 review marketing strategy with Nancy
11 – 11.15 coffee
11.15 – 11.25 call Dave back
11.25 – 11.45 go over report guidelines
11.45 – 12 answer or flag any urgent emails

Phew. I was so exhausted making this up I had to stop, and I'd only got to 12! But this approach does have some advantages:

## GOAL SETTING AND TIME MANAGEMENT

- It is a good way to fit in all your tasks and to prioritise them.
- You may end up using little bits of time that would otherwise be lost.
- If you stuck to your schedule it would make you focus – no more rechecking emails when Dave is expecting your call.
- Scheduling like this is usually more suitable at work than at home and it will help keep work and home separate.
- Spending half an hour every day setting it up will pay dividends through efficiency savings.
- If you're working in a team on event management or something complicated or time-bound, you'll probably work like this out of necessity.
- Michael Hyatt suggests that you pick a maximum of 3 things to do each day – your "big three" – I find scheduling those at a particular time really helps.

*So how do you do it?*

1. Set up one very detailed Small Steps Action List to draw from every day. Add deadlines to it so you know in advance when each task will be completed. Add who's responsible for each task, if appropriate.
2. Before you stop work, schedule your tasks for the next day. Some items will always appear – such as 'answer or flag any urgent emails.' Some will be scheduled by others or appear regularly on certain days of the week – such as 'staff meeting'.
3. Give each task a time slot during your day using a diary that's laid out that way or an app on your phone.
4. Allow some time for unexpected tasks that come up during the day.
5. Keep your hour-by-hour schedule handy on your desk so you can see it.
6. At the end of the day review the schedule and plan the next day.

## 16: BALANCED PLANNING

*What's wrong with this approach?*
- Planning every day in detail takes time and could even lead to burn out.
- It is tempting to plan to use every last little bit of time when – if you think about the rhythm of your day – this doesn't always feel right.
- It is tempting to underestimate how much time each thing takes just to fit everything in, which is demoralising when you don't get everything done.
- You need at least some downtime – a break, a chat with colleagues, a walk to stretch your legs.
- At the same time as avoiding annoyances, it's possible to miss unexpected but useful deviations or distractions or opportunities.
- Sometimes it's better to take the long route.

*Familiar verses unfamiliar*
The more unfamiliar you are with something – a topic, a job, an event you've got to organise – the more carefully you have to plan.

The more familiar you are with something, the more flexible you can be when you plan your time. You can rely on what has become tacit knowledge for you. Remember that it might not be tacit knowledge for people you're dealing with! This mismatch of tacit knowledge can create big communication problems amongst would-be collaborators.

You can test this theory by applying it to anything you know how to do really well. You probably don't have to plan your route to work minute-by-minute anymore, but I bet you planned it carefully on your very first day.

*Getting a feel for a fixed timeframe*
You might have a fixed time period in which to do a task, self-imposed or otherwise. Here are some points to remember:
- You'll learn by doing. Doing something within a fixed timeframe (like teaching a class, for instance) means you'll get a feel for that period of time.

GOAL SETTING AND TIME MANAGEMENT

- Don't be surprised when you need to practise getting used to particular time frames.
- Whether you've promised yourself that you'll work on your Latin grammar or your matchstick model village for an hour every evening, or you're training as a teacher and need to write forty-five-minute lesson plans, or you need to snatch fifteen minutes to write flash fiction in your coffee break, it will take a while to get used to the shape of that time period. But it will either come with practise or you'll discover a more appropriate timeframe for the work.
- Some tasks have externally imposed time frames, some don't.

## Timetabling

Timetabling is an alternative to hour-by-hour planning, and I think it works better in most circumstances. Perhaps because I spend part of my time lecturing in Creative Writing, the idea of *timetabling* a day appeals to me more than a very detailed schedule. I find breaking the day into smaller sessions is useful: early morning, morning, lunchtime, mid-afternoon, late-afternoon, and evening. You then allocate specific tasks to each session. The advantages are:

- It's flexible. If you've scheduled 'work on event with Martha and Harry' on Monday afternoon you can work on any of the specific tasks associated, as long as you know what they are.
- It encourages you to categorise tasks and group them together.
- It doesn't really matter how long each session is. The plan still works.
- Once you start using your timetable, you'll begin to work out how much you can get done during each session, meaning you can tell how much you're likely to get done in future sessions.
- This approach is good for people who are already busy or family members who all have different routines. It's also good for people with a lot to do and a lot of unstructured time, like students or freelancers.

## 16: BALANCED PLANNING

- You can add detailed hour-by-hour or minute-by-minute scheduling as well in places if you need it.
- It's easy to adapt for your own and your family's requirements.
- Remember we looked at rhythms of the year? Watch out for peaks and troughs when using this approach.

*So how do you do it?*
Put aside some time to work on your timetable. Plan together with anyone else involved. What's your time frame? Think about the rhythm of the year. You might want to plan in six-week blocks, for example, or change the plan with the seasons.

1. Set up your Action List. Know when any deadlines are (and who's doing what if you're collaborating).
2. Divide your week into sessions. State roughly what you'll be doing in each session. Do a separate plan for work if you need one.
3. Write it up somewhere you can see it. A white board is ideal, or you could use a pin board, or a planner open on your desk. When you write up your timetable, you can leave space for any specific tasks for particular days or weeks. That's why a whiteboard works so well.

*Including the family*
If you've got kids at home, you could make your timetable big enough and fit the whole family on! That way, everyone gets a reminder of what they and everyone else are doing – no more "but I told you I was going into the office today" – and you can tell at a glance what eating arrangements will need to be for that day. You can see that X will need a packed lunch on Tuesday, Wednesday and Thursday and that Friday will need to be a pizza night because you've planned spend the evening buying birthday presents online. We use a large family calendar for this, but it does mean writing out our commitments more than once as my wife and I also have our own planners.

## GOAL SETTING AND TIME MANAGEMENT

- Use a calendar or wall planner for any big tasks and events.
- Review your to do list with anyone else involved once a week.
- Dividing household tasks fairly makes everyone happier.
- Get kids to help you create a family calendar or pick out photos to go on it.
- Check in with yourself and with your family and work colleagues that the way you've arranged your time is working.

*Adding your goals to your timetable*
Add sessions when you can work on your goals. Imagine you're arranging a date with yourself and write it in your diary or on your calendar. By the way, arranging one appointment with yourself per week is better than unrealistically committing to every evening after work.

### Small steps to balanced time management
*Planning*
Anything big coming up? Having a baby, returning to work, having an operation or medical treatment, starting a new job, getting married, retiring, even Christmas or a holiday all have an impact on your planning. Sometimes it's hard to see beyond them. Build in some time to plan for big things but plan what happens afterwards too:

- Don't hide your plan. Stick it up on the wall or keep it open on your desk.
- Plan for balance. Remember THESE and THEM when you're planning.
- When thinking about your goals, make any extra tasks you've added part of your routine as soon as possible.
- Part of the balanced approach means being balanced in the doing, too. Take breaks, go with the rhythm of the day, stop for a chat or a drink of water, go for a walk.

*Reviewing*
Checking in on your small steps once a week, and once every six to twelve weeks works well.

## 16: BALANCED PLANNING

- How much progress did you make towards your goals? How much THESE and THEM did you include?
- A food, exercise or sleep diary helps with THESE where there's a particular issue.

*Me-management*
Use your journal to record the progress of particular projects and this includes how you're managing your time. For instance, pick just one day. List the things you've managed to achieve and feel good about it. Writing them down makes you realise just how much you've done, rather than berating yourself for what you haven't done. If it didn't go so well, you can record the reasons you were interrupted: snacking, calls from relatives, trips to the shops, the printer running out of ink – naming what got in the way will help you to adjust your plans.

### Balanced planning on trial
*Try this experiment:*
If you're not sure whether timetabling will work for you, then experiment as follows.

- First create your Small Steps Action List if you haven't done so already.
- Draw a week's timetable. Give each early morning, morning, lunchtime, mid-afternoon, late-afternoon, and evening a general title or theme – for one week. If the approach works for you, extend for another week. Journal about the results.

*What's next?*
You've planned for balance. You've thought about the rhythm of the year. You've thought carefully about your goals. You've decided whether an hour-by-hour schedule or a timetable is better for you. Now you've scheduled, stick to it! Or rather: if you can't stick to it, don't worry – simply take the next small step when you get a chance. We're winding things up now, but the spirit of small steps, in the next chapter you'll discover some small adjustments you can make to make it easier to achieve your goals, all in the name of project management.

# Chapter 17: Small Adjustments

**About this chapter**
Small adjustments are small things you can do differently in your day-to-day life that help you to project manage your goals. I suggest you read through this chapter and then spend some time creating systems and routines that work for you. Then make regular project management part of your week. If you are completely snowed under or surrounded by bits of paper or the digital equivalent, and don't know where to start, I recommend adopting David Allen's approach from his book *Getting Things Done*. The final sections of this chapter focus on money and stuff, with some practical tips to help you sort them out!

**Project management**
So, what do I mean by project management? In this context, it means doing whatever it takes to run your life, creating systems and routines to suit, and using scheduled admin time to manage your goals.

*Small Steps Admin*
Be your own PA with the three Rs of small steps admin: regular, reduce, recycle.

1. Regular. Manage your admin tasks – keep a list of them – at least once a week.
    - Remember to break it down and make it easy.
    - Meet weekly with your partner or the whole family to discuss running the household, if relevant.
    - Create a folder and a list of admin tasks related to your goals.
2. Reduce. Decide which tasks need doing and which are unimportant. Keep chipping away at your list and at your filing.

## 17: SMALL ADJUSTMENTS

- Do you really need to keep all of those pieces of paper?
- Make the papers and virtual documents you need regularly easy to find and use.

3. Recycle – don't hoard. Sometimes filing can be an excuse for not letting go. Recycle it instead. Make recycling part of your admin.
   - De-junk and clear the clutter.
   - Create a space for recycling and learn how to recycle confidential information.

## Systems and routines

*Become a system-addict*

You can, and probably already do, use systems and routines at home and at work. Some of these might be subconscious, habitual ways of working. Some are more conscious. As we're looking at small things you can do differently to project manage your goals and fit them into your week, the aim is to become more conscious of the systems and routines we use.

- A system is a pre-planned way of doing or organising something.
- A routine is a pre-planned way of structuring your day or part of it, or another period of time: a week, a term, a year.

*Semi-flexible, simple or straightforward, and shared*

Creating a system or routine or re-evaluating existing ones can help a great deal with time management. For this to work, your systems and routines need to be:

- Semi-flexible. "Semi" because you don't *constantly* reinvent yourself or give in to others who want to override you, and "flexible" because you don't carry on stubbornly when something *needs* to change.
- Simple or straightforward. You need to be able to remember the system and make it habitual. Yes, you can write it out or stick it on the wall but don't make it too complicated.
- Shared with anyone who needs to know.

## GOAL SETTING AND TIME MANAGEMENT

*So how do you do it?*
I wrote the first edition of this book while on maternity leave. I discovered very quickly that, after giving love and providing for your child's basic needs, one of the most important things you can do as a parent of a young child is *anticipate*. It's good advice for time management purposes too. To create a new system or routine:

- Think ahead to what you need to do.
- Set it up.
- Break it down into small steps.
- Make it easy.
- Anticipate interruptions or other demands that might be made on your time.
- Use chunks of time. (Twelve weeks, for example.)
- Consider the peaks and troughs in your year.

*Examples systems and routines*
Here are some examples of the kinds of systems and routines you could invent at home and at work:

- Filing your notes / documents alphabetically so you can access them easily.
- Laying out your room to make the most of the space.
- Inventing an easy way to store post and physical documents you need (an in tray by the front door for example).
- A menu cross-listed with an online shopping list, designed to save money by helping you use up all the food you buy.
- A laundry routine that includes a system for sorting the laundry as you put it in the laundry basket and a system to make it easy to put away clean clothes.
- A way to make sure everyone in the team shares their ideas.
- A calendar to make sure everyone knows which meetings take place when and where.
- A system for communicating to managers the small things that would improve the working environment.

## 17: SMALL ADJUSTMENTS

- A bedtime routine for your children that allows you and your partner one night off a week.

## Filing
*Your Filing System*
It took me a very long time to work out how to make filing work. I had three problems, which I've since learnt are common exasperators:

- Keeping unnecessary bits of paper.
- Maintaining a system that's too complicated.
- Forgetting (or losing) something when it's filed.

I discovered that the answer (as it is with lots of things) is to keep it as simple as possible. Reducing the pile of papers by recycling and filing everything alphabetically solved the problem of losing things. So remember to keep things simple and make it easy to use!

*Practical help with your filing dilemmas*
If you need help with filing physical documents, try this:

1. Get hold of some box files. Consider colour coding if necessary. Find an accessible place to keep them. We now use a set of wicker basket drawers in our hallway – the kind of thing you might put towels in – which makes a handy alternative to box files.
2. Put everything into alphabetical order. 'Alphabetical' is of course open to interpretation. Do the cats' vaccination records go under V for vet or C for cat or P for pet? Go with whatever comes to you first when you think about it – because hopefully you'll file it where you'll end up looking for it!
3. Have one box file dedicated to papers that need to be easy for someone else to find in a difficult situation, such as details of home and life insurance and wills.
4. Any big project with lots of papers associated can have a box file or drawer to itself.
5. As you put everything into alphabetical order, create a recycling

pile for anything you don't need. Use a third 'not sure' pile to review later to avoid a long decision-making process.
6. Use one of the box files for miscellaneous bits such as interesting articles, places to visit and postcards.
7. Recycle the papers you don't need. Do this securely.
8. Keep important papers, insurance documents and wills in a secure fireproof box if possible and / or back them up on your computer.

*Make it easy*
Once your system is set up, you need to use it. To make it easy, I suggest:

1. Have an in tray for things you're working on. (You can have a digital equivalent – a desktop folder for 'current work.')
2. Keep a separate ongoing miscellaneous pile where you can sort things before filing or a 'to sort' folder on your desktop.
3. You might also like to keep a folder for everyday items in easy reach on a bookshelf or in a kitchen drawer. For example, vouchers or money off coupons, info on days out, recipes, letters from your kids' school.
4. Invent a system for your computer folders so the files you need are accessible and easy to find.

## Money
*Saving time and money*
Money can be a real time waster in and of itself, so can worrying about money. Facing up to how you feel about money and dealing with what needs to be done, step-by-step, could save you a fortune as well as saving you time each week.

- Deal with it. Sorting out you money is an important part of admin or being your own PA. Many of us have to sort out our relationship with money too. Long term, this has the effect of making you more efficient, and money admin won't take as much time.
- Plan it. Dealing with money isn't just about how you might use money on a day-to-day basis or how to budget or pay off your

## 17: SMALL ADJUSTMENTS

debts. Planning it puts you in control and again makes it less scary. Again, use small steps. Money management might involve:
- o checking in with your finances once a week,
- o planning for events that take place every year like birthdays and Christmas,
- o saving money by sticking to a budget and following money saving advice,
- o creating small steps for the financial side of your goals,
- o saving for big life events like university, weddings and funerals, and your long-term future.

- Understand it. This is beyond the scope of this book, but another fear-reducing strategy is simply to understand money better. You can do that by talking to a financial advisor, going on a personal finances course, asking for more training at work, brushing up on your maths skills at the local library or reading about money.

### Decluttering your stuff

Throughout this chapter on small adjustments, you might have noticed a theme. In fact, it's a theme that runs right through this book. You're aiming to simplify and to make life easier and one way to do it is by reducing and recycling. The same principles apply to stuff. Decluttering helps us to see – and therefore make the most of – what we have and helps us to create space for our goals. Decluttering saves us time, too, because it's easier to find what we need.

*Use it*

Stop and do this exercise in your journal. We've looked at niggles and bugs, but what if you did the opposite? What if you did a survey of all your stuff and made a note of the things that you use regularly that you really love? What would come out top? Things are useful and it's not always the most expensive things either! We're often told on the one hand that liking stuff is bad and on the other hand – by advertisers everywhere – that we should buy more stuff. This is one way to work your way out of that particular paradox:

- Show some appreciation for the things you use a lot.
- Know what you would do if they went wrong.
- Save for a replacement.
- Know where the manual is kept.
- Make them as easy to use as possible.

*Treasure it*
Some things are precious to us, perhaps because of the memories they hold for us. Some things you'll want to pass on to your loved ones. Consider creating a memory box or displaying items you treasure.

*Donate it or recycle it*
There are charities waiting to take things you don't need off your hands. Charity shops are a starting point. There are also specialist charities that will take away unwanted furniture and give it to families who need it. You could also use freecycle or your local recycling centre.

*Sell it*
There are several ways to sell or give away unwanted stuff, with online marketplaces opening this route up to almost everyone. Here are the main ways to sell:

- Use gumtree, eBay, amazon or one of the other online selling points.
- Car boot sales.
- Specialist markets.
- Nearly new sales.

*What's next?*
You've learnt how to make small adjustments and how to project manage your goals. Next I'll run through some small tools you can use – again in the service of making things easier. Then in the penultimate chapter, you'll discover some small ways to keep in check.

# Chapter 18: Small Tools

### About this chapter
This short chapter gives you small steps and tips to use when it comes to the tools we use in life every day. It covers basic tools (seemingly too trivial to organise but actually a real annoyance-saver), making your computer work for you, and another look at your niggles and bugs and your grateful list.

### Focus on the small stuff
*Basic tools and small annoyances*
Basic tools are very easy to overlook, or to dismiss as trivial, but essential to the Small Steps Method. Keys, pens, notebooks, anything you use a lot could be a basic tool. Do the niggles exercise again, but this time, focus on basic tools that you use every day. Jot down what comes up for you. For instance:

- *"I can never find my keys."*
- *"None of the pens in the pot work."*
- *"I missed J's parent's evening because I lost the letter."*
- *"My pillow's uncomfortable."*
- *"The recycling looks ugly."*
- *"I forget to take my pills."*
- *"I'm supposed to file my receipts somewhere."*

*What can you do about it?*
There are small steps you can take to save yourself time every day and to stop feeling annoyed. Tools that can help with the niggles above include:

- a key basket or pot,
- several notebooks and (working) pens, stored in a central place,

- a pin board / whiteboard / family calendar / everyday 'stuff' drawer.
- A small-enough-to-hide recycling tub for indoors and a recycling system that's part of your daily routine.
- A kid-safe pill box kept near to something you access each morning.
- A basket to collect receipts, or vouchers or letters – or even your keys – as you come in the door.

Have good look at your sleeping area – pillow, alarm clock, bedside table etc. – which of your sleeping tools work for you and which don't?

*The grateful list revisited*
Early on in this book I suggested stopping for a moment every so often and jotting down the things you are grateful for right now. If the small annoyances exercise has left you feeling deflated, try spending a day carrying a small notebook and recording things you are grateful for. It has a powerful effect!

*Is your computer a time-sucker?*
Is your computer sucking the time out of your life? Because a computer is such a fantastic tool it is worth getting it to run as efficiently as possible, by making sure you have the skills needed, but also by sorting out the niggles. Do the niggle exercise again but this time, focus on your computer and your use of the internet. Here are some common niggles:

- *"My computer takes ages to load up."*
- *"My internet service keeps cutting out."*
- *"I don't know how to X and don't know how to find the answer."*
- *"My computer annoys me."*

*De-niggle your computer*
There are small steps you could take to save yourself time. Quick tips that can help with the computer-based niggles above include:

- Getting some technical advice from a local computer firm (where staff usually have more expertise than in the chains).
- Creating back-ups of your work.

## 18: SMALL TOOLS

- Freeing up space or increasing your computer's memory.
- Updating software and operating systems (get advice first).
- Making sure you're on the right internet package for what you want to do.
- If you don't know how to use something on your computer, learning how.

*Are you missing out?*
A while back I used to help beginners learn more about computing and the internet. Many people were eager to learn how to shop online or stay in touch with their family. However, I noticed that some people found computers intensely annoying, were cynical about every move, almost like they were playing chess with a machine, or worried about pressing or clicking on the wrong thing. Usually when they had learnt some basic I.T. skills the suspicion was gone, but for some it hung on. On the other hand, some people have been familiar with computers from an early age but still find them faintly annoying. Everyone has an impatience button somewhere! But computers can help to such an extent that you could be missing out. If this sounds like you, ask yourself *why*? Once you know why you can take some small steps towards doing something about it.

- Is it that the room with the computer in it is cold / noisy / damp / a cupboard?
- Is your desk chair comfortable?
- Is it that it's not running fast enough?
- Is there something you want to make it do, but can't?

## Looking back on your niggles and bugs
*The niggles and bugs exercises revisited*
We've done the niggles and bugs exercise in different ways throughout this book. I suggest that you repeat these regularly, doing the positive and the negative versions of this exercise perhaps a couple of times a year. Here they are again:

1. Write down every small niggle that annoys you, interrupts you, frustrates you or prevents you from doing what you want to do.

Create some small steps to do something about any niggle that's in your control.
2. Keep a bugs diary in a small notebook. Note *anything at all* that bugs you. Create some small steps to help you to de-bug anything in your control.
3. Do a survey of all your stuff, making a note of the things that you use regularly *that you really love*.
4. Note small annoyances, focusing on *basic tools* that you use every day.
5. Do the niggle exercise again but this time, focus on your computer and your use of the internet and social media.
6. Keep a grateful list. We've talked about gratitude a couple of times. One of your lists was specifically about the people in your life.

*What happens next?*
When you review these exercises again and again – including your grateful lists – a funny thing happens:

- After a time, most of the niggles and bugs don't matter anymore.
- Some of the niggles and bugs will have become so habitual you've forgotten there's another way to do it. Awareness helps.
- One or two may stand out to such an extent that you can no longer ignore them.
- The lists of things you love will either prove that something *wasn't* as useful as you thought it was, or it will help you appreciate the enduring usefulness of whatever it is.
- The grateful lists will make you smile and provide inspiration and encouragement as well as helping you put the niggles and bugs in perspective.

*What's next?*
Hopefully those small things that have been annoying you and stopping you from taking small steps are now well on their way to getting sorted. The final two chapters provide you with small ways to keep in check and a list of helpful resources.

# Chapter 19: Small Ways to Keep Check

**About this chapter**
In the opening chapter I gave you some small ways to keep tabs on your progress on your goals and promised you some more. Well, here they are! This short chapter summarises five main ways to keep in check: check in, communicate, collaborate, collect and compost. Use any of these techniques to regularly review, monitor and evaluate your progress, while making a record in your journal. As with all the exercises in this book, only use those that appeal to you.

**Check in**
*Make a date with yourself*
Every so often make a date with yourself. Go somewhere by yourself or simply spend time doing nothing by yourself. If you want to read more about this idea, have a look at Julia Cameron's *The Artist's Way*. I mention her books briefly in chapter seven.

*Make it regular*
When you decide to set goals for yourself and to manage time differently, then it is worth reviewing your goals regularly. Ideally, aim for once a week, then every six weeks and three months.

*Remind yourself*
Find at least three ways to remind yourself of the goals you've set or the time management strategies you want to try. For example:

- Put it in view in more than once place: the fridge, calendar, noticeboard or whiteboard.
- Block out space in your diary.
- Use your phone to remind you.

GOAL SETTING AND TIME MANAGEMENT

*Set it up in advance*
In the heat of the moment, it may be difficult to stick to what we've decided to do. Instead set up a way of doing it in advance and stick to it. Even better, make it habitual.

*Remember to make it easy*
The easier you make the process, the more likely you are to do it. Make your steps small enough so that they seem simple enough to achieve. If in doubt set yourself one task, achievable in one session (morning, evening or afternoon) and that could be built into your day.

**Communicate**
*Talk to others, talk to yourself*
Remember to communicate your ideas, worries, questions and thought processes about your goals and your new time management strategies. Obviously this is important if others are involved. Saying something out loud or writing it down is also a way of thinking or communicating with yourself. You can do this by:

- Discussing ideas informally: make time to chat when the pressure is off and without applying any pressure yourself.
- Holding meetings: bring the interested parties together, use an agenda and create a list of action points, with deadlines. Make sure everyone is heard.
- Try teaching others. You end up explaining it to yourself as well and you'll learn about the subject as your research it.
- Journaling. We've been doing this throughout. The process of writing a journal allows you to communicate how you really feel about something and allows your brain the space to come up with some solutions to problems.
- Blogging, as a form of accountability and a record of your progress / process. In some cases, you can grow an online following this way too.

## 19: SMALL WAYS TO KEEP CHECK

### Collaborate
*Groups get you going*
Previously we talked about the importance of support when planning to achieve your goals. Collaboration with others is also a good way to keep check. Groups are motivating. You can provide support to others, and they can support you. This works for direct support (like a Quit Smoking group) or indirect support (the friendship provided by a club or society). Collaborating with a group of people on your project will provide a number of people to call you up any time your progress stalls.

### Collect
*The collecting process*
Another small way to keep in check is to make time to collect together any of the following information:

- equipment
- articles
- images
- noticeboard items: either inspirational or practical ones

Collect these together in a box file, scrapbook or on a noticeboard. The process of collecting these things together keeps you thinking about and reviewing your progress. Remember the section on confirmation bias? You get what you focus on!

### Compost
*Garden time revisited*
I've already said that sometimes working toward your goals is like gardening. It takes time to make a garden. Likewise, you're preparing the ground for your goals, putting in your plants and tending them as they grow. When you've researched what it takes to achieve your goals, when you've thought about the changes you can make to manage time more effectively, give it time, especially if you want a particular technique to become second nature. Give yourself time to:

## GOAL SETTING AND TIME MANAGEMENT

- let it sink in
- let it mature.

It helps if you combine this kind of composting with journaling or other kinds of 'mulling time'. Take time out, go on walks, spend time with those you love, or do things with your hands if you usually work with your head.

*What's next?*

Thanks for coming with me on this exploration of goal setting and time management strategies. I hope you've found some useful tools in this section that you can implement quickly and that will help you to organise your life a little bit more, enough to fit in some of those small steps. I'd love to know how you get on, so please get in touch. In the next chapter, I've listed the resources I've mentioned as we've gone along and given references for the concepts and ideas I've discussed. Happy goal setting – keep taking small steps!

# Chapter 20: Bibliography and Resources

## Resources
Here are some books and articles to read, plus other resources, in case you'd like to find out more about a particular topic.

### How to find me
Blog: https://www.louisetondeur.co.uk/blog/
Twitter: https://twitter.com/louisetondeur
I am slowly adding to a list of books on goal setting and time management at: https://uk.bookshop.org/shop/LouiseTondeur

### Apps
Brain FM: https://www.brain.fm/
Evernote: https://evernote.com/
Things (available through your app store)

### Circadian rhythms
Clear, James, *Atomic Habits* (Random House Business) 2018
Hyatt, Michael, *Living Forward* (Baker Books) 2016
Milkman, Katy, *How to Change* (Vermilion) 2022
Pink, Daniel H., *When* (Canongate) 2019
The Very Well Health on circadian rhythms and sleep: https://www.verywellhealth.com/the-science-of-circadian-rhythms-3014832
Wiseman, Richard, *Night School* Pan (2015)

### Cognitive biases
What are cognitive biases? From the Very Well Mind website: https://www.verywellmind.com/what-is-a-cognitive-bias-2794963
What is negativity bias? From the Very Well Mind website: https://www.verywellmind.com/negative-bias-4589618

GOAL SETTING AND TIME MANAGEMENT

## Decluttering

Leeds, Regina, *One Year to an Organized Life: From Your Closets to Your Finances* (Da Capo Lifelong) 2008

Silverthorn, Vicky, *Start with Your Sock Drawer: The Simple Guide to Living a Less Cluttered Life* (Sphere) 2016

## Focus / avoiding distraction

Eyal, Nir *Indistractable* (Bloomsbury ) 2020
Hanh, Thich Nhat, *How to Focus* (Penguin) 2022
Hari, Johann, *Stolen Focus* (Bloomsbury ) 2023
Hyatt, Michael, *Free to Focus* (Baker Books) 2019
Keller, Gary, *The One Thing*. (John Murray) 2014
Levitin, Daniel, *The Organised Mind* (Penguin ) 2015
Newport, Cal, *Deep Work* (Piatkus) 2016

## Goal Setting

James Clear on Warren Buffett 5/25 rule: https://jamesclear.com/buffett-focus

Ditzler, Jinny, *Your Best Year Yet: Make the Next 12 Months Your Best Ever* (Harper Element) 2006

Hyatt, Michael, *Living Forward* (Baker Books) 2016

Hyatt, Michael, *Your Best Year Ever* (Baker Books) 2018

Tracy, Brian, *Goals: How to Get Everything You Want Faster Than You Ever Thought Possible* (Berrett-Koehler) 2010

The Wheel of Life: https://www.thecoachingtoolscompany.com/wheel-of-life-complete-guide-everything-you-need-to-know/

## To do lists

There are suggestions in Ronni Eisenberg's book *Organise Yourself* (2006).

If you'd like an alternative system for handling to do lists, have a look at Mark Forster's books, under 'time management'.

Michael Hyatt's blog includes to-do list inspiration, for instance: https://fullfocus.co/before-you-create-a-to-do-list/

Online to do lists include: https://www.rememberthemilk.com/ Other digital solutions are listed under 'Apps.'

20: BIBLIOGRAPHY AND RESOURCES

## Gratitude

Michael Hyatt discusses the importance of gratitude in chapter 6 of *Your Best Year Ever* (2018).
Here's an article on gratitude from the Greater Good Center at Berkeley: https://greatergood.berkeley.edu/article/item/is_gratitude_the_path_to_better_world

## Habits / habits of success

Covey, Stephen, *The 7 Habits of Highly Effective People* (Simon and Schuster) 2004
Currey, Mason, *Daily Rituals* (Picador) 2020
Currey, Mason, *Daily Rituals: Women at Work* (Picador) 2020
Clear, James, *Atomic Habits* (Random House Business) 2018
Mason Currey's blog 'Daily Routines': https://dailyroutines.typepad.com/
Duhigg, Charles, *The Power of Habit* (Penguin) 2013
Gladwell, Malcolm, *Outliers: The Story of Success* (Penguin) 2009
Kelsey, Robert, *What's Stopping You? Why Smart People Don't Always Reach Their Potential and How You Can* (Capstone) 2011
Milkman, Katy, *How to Change* (Vermilion) 2022
Morland, Polly, *Metamorphosis: How and Why We Change* (Profile Books) 2016
Ratey, Nancy, *The Disorganized Mind* (St. Martin's Griffin) 2008
Swoboda, Kate *The Courage Habit* (New Harbinger) 2018

## Happiness

Burkeman, Oliver, *The Antidote: Happiness for People Who Can't Stand Positive Thinking* (Vintage 2018)
Tolle, Eckhart *The Power of Now* (Yellow Kite) 2001
The Very Well Mind website on what sciences knows about being happy. https://www.verywellmind.com/what-is-happiness-4869755

## Happiness Pioneers

*Tara Brach*
Brach, Tara, *Radical Acceptance* (Bantam) 2004.
Website: http://tarabrach.com
Tara Brach's Meditation on communicating with your future self is here: https://youtu.be/g5XXQPQofxk

GOAL SETTING AND TIME MANAGEMENT

*Brené Brown*
Brown, Brené, *The Gifts of Imperfection* (Hazelden) 2022
Brown, Brené, *Daring Greatly*. (Penguin 2015)
Website: https://brenebrown.com/

*Ed Diener*
Biswas-Diener, Robert and Diener, Ed, *Happiness: Unlocking the Mysteries of Psychological Wealth* (Wiley-Blackwell) 2008

*Dan Harris*
Harris, Dan, *10% Happier* (Yellow Kite) 2017
Website: https://www.tenpercent.com/
See also: Oren Jay Sofer: https://www.orenjaysofer.com/ and Sebene Selassie: https://www.sebeneselassie.com/

*Russ Harris*
Harris, Russ, *The Happiness Trap* (Robinson) 2022
Website: https://thehappinesstrap.com/my-story/

*Dacher Keltner*
Keltner, Dacher, *Born to Be Good: The Science of a Meaningful Life.* (Norton) 2010.
Website: https://greatergood.berkeley.edu/

*Kristin Neff*
Germer, Christopher and Kristin Neff, *The Mindful Self-Compassion Workbook* (Guilford Press) 2018
Website: https://self-compassion.org/

*Laurie Santos*
The Science of Well-Being (free course) https://www.coursera.org/learn/the-science-of-well-being

*Martin Seligman*
Seligman, Martin E.P., *Authentic Happiness: Using the New Positive Psychology to Realise Your Potential for Lasting Fulfilment* (Nicholas Brealey) 2003

20: BIBLIOGRAPHY AND RESOURCES

## Journaling

'Getting into Writing', in Bolton, Gillie, Field, Victoria, and Thompson, Kate, *Writing Routes: A Resource Handbook of Therapeutic Writing* (Jessica Kingsley Publishers) 2010, pages 17–34.
Cameron, Julia, *The Artist's Way* (Pan) 2011. http://juliacameronlive.com
Michael Hyatt produces planners and journals that complement his books, especially *Living Forward* (2016).
Find out more about therapeutic writing at: https://www.lapidus.org.uk/

## Journey-focused

Burkeman, Oliver, *Four Thousand Weeks* (Vintage) 2022
Brach, Tara, *Radical Acceptance* (Bantam ) 2004. Website: http://tarabrach.com
Cameron, Julia, *The Artist's Way* (Pan) 2011 and *The Sound of Paper* (Penguin) 2006.
Cameron, Julia *Write for Life* (Souvenir ) 2023. Website: http://juliacameronlive.com
Kornfield, Jack, *After the Ecstasy, the Laundry: How the Heart Grows Wise on the Spiritual Path* (Bantam) 2001
Kornfield, Jack, *A Path with Heart* (Rider) 2002
Shapiro, Stephen M., *Goal-Free Living: How to Have the Life You Want Now* (John Wiley) 2006.
Life is not a journey by Alan Watt: https://www.youtube.com/watch?v=qHnIJeE3LAI

## Life roles or the whole self

Beck, Martha, *Finding Your Way in a Wild New World* (Piatkus) 2012
Burton, Kate, *Live Life, Love Work* (Capstone) 2010
Buzan, Tony, 'Mind maps for self-analysis', in *The Mind Map Book: Unlock Your Creativity, Boost Your Memory, Change Your Life* (BBC Active) 2009, pp. 119–127. http://www.thinkbuzan.com/uk/
Castillo, Brooke, *Self-Coaching 101* (Futures) 2008
Ditzler, Jinny, *Your Best Year Yet: Make the Next 12 Months Your Best Ever* (Harper Element) 2006
Hyatt, Michael, *Living Forward* (Baker Books) 2016
Mayne, Brian, *Goal Mapping: How to Turn Your Dreams into Realities* (Watkins) 2006

St. John, Noah, *The Book of Affirmations* (Hay House) 2013)
The Wheel of Life: https://www.thecoachingtoolscompany.com/wheel-of-life-complete-guide-everything-you-need-to-know/

## Mistakes and perseverance / performance

Duckworth, Angela, *Grit: Why Passion and Resilience are the Secrets to Success* (Vermilion) 2017
Dweck, Carol S., *Mindset: How You Can Fulfil Your Potential* (Robinson) 2012
Ericsson, Anders and Robert Pool, *Peak: How All of Us Can Achieve Extraordinary Things* (Vintage) 2017
Gladwell, Malcolm , *Outliers: The Story of Success* (Penguin) 2009
Harford, Tim, *Adapt: Why Success Always Starts with Failure* (Abacus) 2011
Harford, Tim, *Messy: How to Be Creative and Resilient in a Tidy-Minded World* (Abacus) 2018
Milkman, Katy, *How to Change* (Vermilion) 2022
Syed, Matthew, *Dare to Be You* (Wren & Rook) 2020
Syed, Matthew, *You are Awesome* (Wren & Rook) 2018
Syed, Matthew, *Bounce: The Myth of Talent and the Power of Practice* (Fourth Estate) 2011

## Money

Pine, Karen J., and Gnessen, Simonne, *Sheconomics* (Headline) 2009
Stanny, Barbara, *Overcoming Underearning: A Five-Step Plan to a Richer Life* (Harper Business) 2019

## Motivation

Rubin, Gretchen, *The Four Tendencies* (Two Roads) 2018. Discover your tendency by taking the quiz on Rubin's website. https://gretchenrubin.com/books/the-four-tendencies/
Oliver Burkeman's on why you shouldn't "wait until you feel like doing something": https://www.psychologytoday.com/gb/blog/the-antidote/201211/cranky-pessimists-guide-getting-things-done

20: BIBLIOGRAPHY AND RESOURCES

## Niggles and bugs

The inspiration for the practical niggles and bugs exercises was Oliver Burkeman's column 'Mild Irritation', *Guardian*, 10th March 2007 and is available from: www.guardian.co.uk/lifeandstyle/2007/mar/10/weekend.oliverburkeman

## Organisation

Allen, David, *Getting Things Done: How to Achieve Stress-free Productivity* (Piatkus) 2002. Website: http://www.davidco.com/about-gtd
Eisenberg, Ronni, *Organise Yourself* (Piatkus) 2006

## Podcasts

Brené Brown's podcasts are detailed on her website at: https://brenebrown.com/
Brooke Castillo talks about Monday hour one in her podcast at: https://www.youtube.com/watch?v=4si8E9vsGVk
Angela Duckworth hosts *No Stupid Questions*.
Dan Harris hosts *10% Happier*
Dacher Keltner hosts *The Science of Happiness*
*The Happiness Lab* hosted by Dr Laurie Santos

## Prioritising

Read the blog post about Warren Buffett 5/25 rule on James Clear's website: https://jamesclear.com/buffett-focus

## Productivity, work or sales goals

Duffield-Thomas, Denise *Chillpreneur* (Hay House) 2020
Ferriss, Tim, *The 4-Hour Workweek* (Vermilion) 2011
Gullibeau, Chris, *Side-Hustle* (Macmillan) 2017
Gullibeau, Chris, *$100 Start Up* (Macmillan) 2012
Gullibeau, Chris, *The Art of Non-Conformity* (Turnaround) 2011
Hyatt, Michael, *Your Best Year Ever* (Baker Books) 2018
Sinek, Simon, *Start With Why* (Penguin) 2011
Johnson, Spencer, *Who Moved My Cheese: An Amazing Way to Deal with Change in Your Work and in Your Life* (Vermilion) 1999.
Pink, Daniel H.,*To Sell is Human* (Canongate) 2013
Tracy, Brian, *Goals: How to Get Everything You Want Faster Than You Ever Thought Possible* (Berrett-Koehler) 2010

GOAL SETTING AND TIME MANAGEMENT

Tracy, Brian, *Eat That Frog: 21 Great Ways To Stop Procrastinating and Get More Done In Less Time* (Collins Business) 2012
Ziglar, Zig, *Top Performance: How to Develop Excellence in Yourself and Others* (Revell) 2004

## Recycling / freebie sites

www.ilovefreegle.org
http://uk.freecycle.org/
Here's an interesting article about how to use freebie sites: http://www.moneysavingexpert.com/shopping/freecycle

## Scheduling

Vanderkam, Laura, *I Know How She Does It: How Successful Women Make the Most of Their Time* (Portfolio) 2015

## Skills exchange / time bank schemes

Article from the Love Money website on how to swap your skills using time bank schemes: https://www.lovemoney.com/news/62268/skills-exchange-swap-trading-time-bank

## Sleep

The New Scientist offers a free course on the Science of Sleep: https://academy.newscientist.com/courses/science-of-sleep-and-dreams
*Night School* by Richard Wiseman (2015) was one of the first books I read about sleep science.

## SMART goal setting

Here's a typical rendition of the SMART goals technique from Brian Tracy's blog: https://www.briantracy.com/blog/personal-success/smart-goals-action-plan/
Michael Hyatt's version of the SMARTER goals acronym is here: https://fullfocus.co/goal-setting/ – I like how he makes the first 'r' 'risky' the 'e' 'exciting'!
Find out more about the history of SMART goals here: https://www.projectsmart.co.uk/smart-goals/brief-history-of-smart-goals.php

## 20: BIBLIOGRAPHY AND RESOURCES

### Time management

Allen, David, *Getting Things Done: How to Achieve Stress-free Productivity* (Piatkus) 2002. Website: http://www.davidco.com/about-gtd

Bregman, Peter, *18 Minutes: Find Your Focus, Master Distraction and Get the Right Things Done* (Orion) 2012

Burkeman, Oliver, 'How to Rule the Office' and 'How to Get More Done' in *Help: How to Become Slightly Happier and Get a Bit More Done*, (Cannongate), pp. 93–140.

Cirillo, Francesco *The Pomodoro Technique* (Lulu.com) 2009 Available to download for free from: www.pomodorotechnique.com

Eisenberg, Ronni, *Organise Yourself* (Piatkus) 2006

Forster, Mark, *Do it Tomorrow and Other Secrets of Time Management* (Hodder and Stoughton) 2006 and *Get Everything Done and Still Have Time to Play* (Hodder and Stoughton) 2000.

Ferriss, Tim, *The 4-Hour Workweek* (Vermilion) 2011

Tondeur, Louise, *Find Time to Write* (Small Steps) 2022

The Kettle Test: https://www.louisetondeur.co.uk/find-time-to-write-with-the-kettle-test/

### Values

James Clear has a list of values on his website: https://jamesclear.com/core-values

### Volunteering

NCVO: https://www.ncvo.org.uk/get-involved/volunteering/want-to-volunteer/

### Writing

Cameron, Julia *Write for Life* (Souvenir ) 2023. Website: http://juliacameronlive.com

Ingermanson, Randy and Peter Economy *Writing Fiction For Dummies* (John Wiley) 2009

Tondeur, Louise, *How to Write a Novel and Get It Published* (Small Steps) 2022.

Tondeur, Louise, *Find Time to Write* (Small Steps) 2022

## Sources

### Chapter 1
*Maslow's Pyramid*
Atkinson, Sam et al, eds., *The Psychology Book*, (Dorling Kindersly) 2012, p. 138–139.
Maslow, Abraham, 'A theory of human motivation', *Psychological Review*, No. 50, 1943, pages 370–96.

*Mindset*
Dweck, Carol S., *Mindset: How You Can Fulfil Your Potential* (Robinson) 2012. For an example of Dweck's other work, see *Handbook of Competence and Motivation*, edited with Andrew J. Elliot (Guilford) 2005

### Chapter 2
*Convergent / divergent thinking:*
Atkinson, Sam et al, eds., *The Psychology Book*, (Dorling Kindersly) 2012, p. 305.
J.P. Guilford, 'Traits of creativity' in P.E. Vernon (ed.), *Creativity* (Penguin) 1970.

### Chapter 4
Christakis, Nicholas and Fowler, James 'The Strength of Weak Ties' in *Connected: The Amazing Power of Social Networks and How They Shape Our Lives* (Harper Press) 2011, pp. 156–163. See also: Gladwell, Malcolm, *Tipping Point* (Abacus) 2002
Colman, Andrew, *A Dictionary of Psychology* (Oxford Reference) 2009.
Miller, Amber, 'Experience: I went into labour after running a marathon.' 16th June 2017, *Guardian*. Available at: https://www.theguardian.com/lifeandstyle/2017/jun/16/experience-went-into-labour-after-running-marathon
Water Aid website: www.wateraid.org/uk/about_us/default.asp
Wikipedia's list of cognitive biases: http://en.wikipedia.org/wiki/List_of_cognitive_biases
Winstanley, Julie, *Key Concepts in Psychology* (Palgrave) 2006
'Woman gives birth hours after running Chicago Marathon', *BBC News website*, 11th October 2011 www.bbc.co.uk/news/world-us-canada-15251624

20: BIBLIOGRAPHY AND RESOURCES

## Chapter 5

The Alcoholic's Prayer (or Serenity Prayer) was attributed to Reinhold Niebuhr in Sifton, Elisabeth, *The Serenity Prayer: Faith and Politics in Times of Peace and War* (Norton) 2004.
Murray, W. H., *The Scottish Himalayan Expedition* (Dent) 1951.
You can find the Arvon Foundation's courses listed here: https://www.arvon.org/

## Chapter 6

*On definitions of happiness and happiness measures*
Anielski, Mark, *The Economics of Happiness: Building Genuine Wealth* (New Society) 2007.
Better Life Index. The OECD's Better Life Index is at: http://oecdbetterlifeindex.org/about/better-life-initiative/ (OECD stands for the Organisation for Economic Co-operation and Development.)
Nauert, Rick, 'Happiness Tied to Choice and Autonomy, Not Money', Psych Central, June 2011. http://psychcentral.com/news/2011/06/15/some-items-more-important-than-money-for-happiness/26945.html
Office for National Statistics, 'Initial investigation into Subjective Well-being from the Opinions Survey' ONS website, 1st December 2011 http://tinyurl.com/ONSwellbeingsurvey. See also:_www.ons.gov.uk/peoplepopulationandcommunity/wellbeing_
Rudin, Mike, 'The Science of Happiness', *BBC News website*, 2006 http://news.bbc.co.uk/1/hi/programmes/happiness_formula/4783836.stm
Salmansohn, Karen, 'The No. 1 Contributor to Happiness: Why/how to regain your autonomy to increase your joy!' *Psychology Today website*, 2011. www.psychologytoday.com/blog/bouncing-back/201106/the-no-1-contributor-happiness

*On teams, social dynamics and altruism*
Brown, Michael, Brown, R Stephanie L., Penner, Louis A., *Moving Beyond Self-Interest: Perspectives from Evolutionary Biology, Neuroscience, and the Social Sciences*, OUP USA, 2011
Christakis, Nicholas and Fowler, James *Connected: The Amazing Power of Social Networks and How They Shape Our Lives* (Harper Press) 2011

Lewis, Sarah, *Positive Psychology at Work: How Positive Leadership and Appreciative Inquiry Create Inspiring Organizations* (Wiley-Blackwell) 2011

## Chapter 8
*Eating healthily*
NHS website: https://www.nhs.uk/healthier-families/
Natalie Savona's *The Kitchen Shrink: Foods and Recipes for a Healthy Mind* (Duncan Baird ) 2004.

*Quitting Smoking*
NHS website: https://www.nhs.uk/better-health/quit-smoking/

## Chapter 11
*Eight secrets*
"The eight secrets of goal-free living" are used to structure Shapiro, Stephen M., *Goal-Free Living: How to Have the Life You Want Now* (John Wiley) 2006.

## Chapter 13
Sophie Hannah's Dream Author: https://dreamauthorcoaching.com/

## Chapter 14
*The Snowflake method*
Ingermanson, Randy and Peter Economy *Writing Fiction For Dummies* (John Wiley) 2009

*Essay Writing example*
Livi-Bacci's, Massimo, *A Concise History of World Population* (Wiley-Blackwell) 2012
Rosenberg, Charles E., *The Cholera Years: United States in the Years 1832, 1849 and 1866* (University of Chicago) 1987

## Chapter 19
*Julia Cameron on 'Artists' Dates'*
See: *The Artist's Way* (Pan) 2011 and *The Sound of Paper* (Penguin) 2006 and the tools on her website at: http://juliacameronlive.com

Lou worked as a Drama teacher before doing an MA in Creative Writing at The University of East Anglia. She published two novels with Headline Review called *The Water's Edge* and *The Haven Home for Delinquent Girls*, then wrote a PhD, started a family, and became a Creative Writing lecturer. Since then, she has published several books, articles, stories and poetry. She currently lectures part-time for the Open University and the University of Brighton and writes for (at least some of) the rest of the week. Lou grew up in Bournemouth and lived in London for nearly twenty years. She now lives near Brighton with her wife and son and two black cats and blogs at: www.louisetondeur.co.uk/blog.